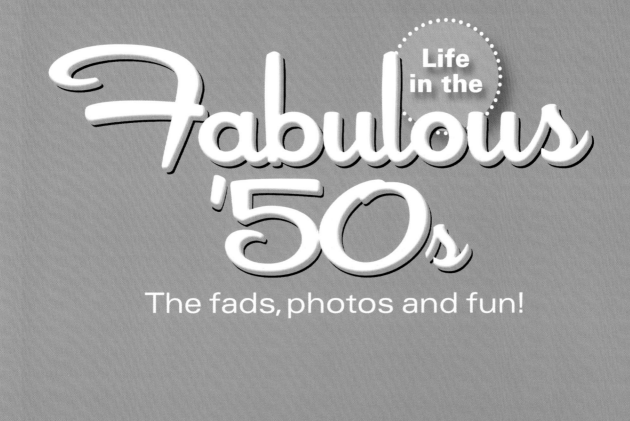

Life
in the

Fabulous '50s

The fads, photos and fun!

table of contents

Home & Garden

Karol K. Nickell VP and Editor-in-Chief
Heather Lamb Executive Editor
Rachael Liska Product Development Editor
Sharon K. Nelson Creative Director

Life in the Fabulous '50s

Dan Bishop, Angela Packer Art Directors
**Jacqueline DuPont, Julie Kastello,
Vanessa Torweihe, Kenneth Wysocky**
Contributors
Joanne Weintraub Copy Editor
Kathleen Ann Bergant Proofreader
Dena Ahlers Layout Designer
Trudi Bellin Photo Coordinator
Mary Ann Koebernik Assistant Photo Coordinator

Bettina Miller Editor, *Reminisce*
Cheryl A. Michalek Art Director, *Reminisce*
John Burlingham Associate Editor, *Reminisce*
Blanche Comiskey, Melody Trick
Editorial Assistants, *Reminisce*

Lisa Karpinski CMO, Home & Garden
Mark Andersen CFO, Home & Garden

The Reader's Digest Association, Inc.

Mary G. Berner President and Chief Executive Officer
Alyce C. Alston President, Home & Garden
and Health & Wellness
Amy J. Radin SVP, Chief Marketing Officer
Dawn M. Zier President, Global Consumer Marketing
and CEO, Direct Holdings

Reminisce Books

© 2009 Reiman Media Group, Inc.
5400 S. 60th St., Greendale WI 53129-1404

International Standard Book Number:
0-89821-757-1
978-0-89821-757-5

Library of Congress Control Number: 2009930798

On the Cover: Classic car by Ian Shaw/Alamy

For additional copies of this book
or information on other books, write:
Reminisce Customer Service, P.O. Box 5294,
Harlan IA 53593-0794;
call toll-free: 1-800/344-6913;
E-mail: rpsubscustomercare@custhelp.com.
Visit our Web site at *Reminisce*.com

Welcome back to a magical decade...

to life in the fabulous '50s as it really was. This one-of-a-kind book comes to you from the editors of *Reminisce*, the memories-magazine dedicated to "bringing back the good times." Since premiering in 1991, *Reminisce* has grown to become America's No. 1 nostalgia publication by delighting our nearly 1.2 million readers with real-life stories and photos from the past. Each issue is filled with heartfelt and hilarious personal accounts that have been submitted by folks just like you! The same care and commitment went into putting this book together, and we're thrilled to devote an entire book to such a joyful era.

Fascination with the 1950s seems to grow stronger as the years go by. As one of our country's most optimistic and culturally rich decades, it brought us happy times at the backyard barbecue, innovations like the polio vaccine and mind-boggling challenges like the race into space. New fads, fashions and entertainment filled the '50s: poodle skirts, Hula-hoops and coonskin caps, as the early days of television brought music, comedy and drama right into our living rooms as never before. And those cars! The styles and chrome and colors—it's no wonder Sunday drives became so popular. Family life was apple-pie idyllic, and our readers' memories of these events and simple togetherness are compelling and real.

One of my favorite stories from this book is Janet Apuzzo's account of life in the 'burbs, when Mom stayed home and Dad made the daily commute to work, so proud to return each evening to a house with a yard and nice neighbors. "Life was simple and innocent then," Janet says. "Eating watermelon in the summer, wearing baby-doll pajamas on a hot night, dressing my Barbie...I miss those days."

We hear from readers that each issue of *Reminisce* brings friends and family together. Over our pages, past days, personal milestones and family memories are shared. We also want this book to help bring generations together. Because we believe it's so important to record real-life nostalgia, we've included journaling spots in each chapter for you to add your own memories. This can create a wonderful keepsake for children and grandchildren. And if you're like many of our younger readers who love '50s memories but are too young to have experienced those years, you can use these journaling areas to record memories from your parents or grandparents—or simply write down your own thoughts of what you would have liked most, had you lived back then.

The '50s were fabulous because of the people who lived them. We hope their stories—told so beautifully in this book—will bring back your personal memories, make you laugh out loud, tear up in happiness and share them with a kindred spirit.

Bettina Miller

Bettina Miller
Editor, *Reminisce* magazine

1950–1959:
A Retrospective

There has perhaps never been a decade as distinctive as the 1950s. The fashions, the food, the fads, the faces—all of it iconic Americana in the making. Drive-ins, Hula-hoops, James Dean and Elvis competed for attention with the Korean War, the emergence of Fidel Castro, the space race and the rise of suburbia.

So before you turn the page to look ahead, take a moment and look back at the events that made the '50s such a compelling—and fabulous—time in history.

1950

It's a year of firsts—television remote controls, Minute Rice and Diners Club cards are rolled out to the delight of families everywhere.

▲ **FEBRUARY** Walt Disney releases *Cinderella*, while the number of drive-in movie theaters reaches an impressive 2,200.

APRIL The Minneapolis Lakers win their second NBA championship and begin the Lakers' legacy, with 25 championship titles between the Minneapolis Lakers and the Los Angeles Lakers from 1949 to 2000.

▲ **JUNE** President Harry Truman authorizes the use of American troops to repel the North Korean invasion of South Korea, marking the beginning of the Korean War and a decade of bomb fear.

▶ **OCTOBER** Charles Schulz introduces Charlie Brown to America as the *Peanuts* comic strip debuts.

1951

◀ **AUGUST** J.D. Salinger publishes *Catcher in the Rye*.

▼ **OCTOBER** Sports fans listen to "the shot heard 'round the world" as the Brooklyn Dodgers and New York Giants race for the National League pennant. CBS introduces both the eye logo and *I Love Lucy* to television audiences. One of America's first malls, Shoppers World, opens in Framingham, Massachusetts.

▲ **NOVEMBER** The first military exercises for nuclear war are held in the Nevada desert.

1952

Revolutionary icons introduced this year: Mr. Potato Head, Frosted Flakes' "Tony the Tiger" and Les Paul's solid-body Gibson guitar.

▲ FEBRUARY After the death of King George VI, England sees the beginning of the long reign of his older daughter, Elizabeth II.

APRIL The United States ends the occupation of Japan.

▼ JULY Argentina's most influential figure, Eva Peron, dies of cancer at the age of 33.

NOVEMBER Virginia Tighe, a Colorado homemaker, claims to have vivid recollections of a prior life as a 19th-century Irish lass named Bridey Murphy during a recorded hypnotic session.

1953

▲ JANUARY Dwight D. Eisenhower takes office as the first Republican president in 20 years.

MARCH The 25th Academy Awards is the first ceremony broadcast on television. Soviet leader Joseph Stalin dies of a stroke.

▲ JUNE General Motors introduces the Chevrolet Corvette. The same month, 36-year-old senator John F. Kennedy announces his engagement to 23-year-old debutante Jacqueline Bouvier.

▶ JULY Marilyn Monroe stars in *Gentlemen Prefer Blondes* and sings the hit song *Diamonds Are a Girl's Best Friend*.

▼ DECEMBER Hugh Hefner publishes the first issue of *Playboy*.

1954

The boom age begins as the New York Stock Exchange sees its most active trading year since 1933. Over $3 billion is spent on new construction across the country.

▲ **APRIL** Hank Aaron breaks into the Milwaukee Braves' lineup.

▲ **JUNE** President Eisenhower modifies the Pledge of Allegiance from "one nation indivisible" to "one nation, under God, indivisible."

▼ **SEPTEMBER** Famous fictional collie *Lassie* debuts on television.

▼ **DECEMBER** Disney's *Davy Crockett* becomes a national craze. The phrases "do-it-yourself" and "sci-fi" are coined.

Davy Crockett

1955

▲ **APRIL** English Prime Minister Sir Winston Churchill resigns. Albert Einstein, one of the greatest scientific minds of all time, dies in Princeton, New Jersey.

▲ **JULY** Austria regains independence after years of occupation before and after World War II. Disneyland opens in California.

▲ **SEPTEMBER** Rising screen actor and American legend James Dean dies in a car accident in Los Angeles.

▶ **OCTOBER** The Brooklyn Dodgers win their first World Series after losing the previous 5 out of 7 against the New York Yankees. Ford challenges the Chevrolet Corvette with the Thunderbird.

▼ **DECEMBER** Rosa Lee Parks refuses to give up her seat and fuels the Montgomery Bus Boycott in Alabama.

Ford Thunderbird

Bus Boycott

1950–1959: A Retrospective

Rocky Marciano

1956

▲ **APRIL** Elvis Presley hits record store shelves and "Elvis mania" begins. Boxer Rocky Marciano retires as the only undefeated heavyweight champion in boxing history. Iconic actress Grace Kelly marries Prince Rainier III of Monaco.

JUNE The Federal-Aid Highway Act frees $25 billion to build 41,000 miles of interstate highways.

▼ **JULY** The Ringling Bros. and Barnum & Bailey Circus performs its last tent extravaganza in Pittsburgh. Thereafter, shows are in arenas.

▼ **SEPTEMBER** The Summer Olympic Games are held in the fall for the first time in Melbourne, Australia.

NOVEMBER The long-running television game show *The Price Is Right* premieres.

Summer Olympics

1957

Little Rock Nine

▲ 1957 inventions include the transistorized pacemaker, artificial heart, pocket-sized radio and Frisbee.

▲ **AUGUST** Dick Clark introduces *American Bandstand*.

▲ **SEPTEMBER** President Eisenhower sends federal troops and places the Arkansas National Guard under federal command when the "Little Rock Nine" bravely attempt to attend Little Rock Central High School in Arkansas after an angry white mob breaks out in violent protest.

▼ **OCTOBER** Russia begins the space race by launching the first Earth-orbiting satellite, *Sputnik 1*. Someone other than the Brooklyn Dodgers takes on the New York Yankees in the World Series, with the Milwaukee Braves winning 4–3. *Leave It to Beaver* premieres on CBS.

Sputnik 1

Life in the Fabulous '50s

Bobby Fischer

Buddy Holly

Fidel Castro

1958

1959

This year, the Hula-hoop and Rice-a-Roni—the San Francisco treat—are introduced.

▲ **JANUARY** The United States launches its first satellite, *Explorer I*, to compete with the Russian *Sputniks*. Fourteen-year-old whiz Bobby Fischer wins the U.S. Chess Championship.

▲ **APRIL** The Brooklyn Dodgers play their first game as the Los Angeles Dodgers at the Los Angeles Memorial Coliseum.

JUNE Charles de Gaulle comes out of retirement to become France's prime minister before being elected president.

JULY Congress creates NASA.

AUGUST The United States Air Force Academy opens in Colorado Springs, Colorado.

▲ **OCTOBER** Pope John XXIII is elected after the death of Pope Pius XII. The New York Yankees reclaim their glory with a World Series win over the Milwaukee Braves.

▶ **DECEMBER**
Johnny Unitas and the Baltimore Colts beat the New York Giants, 23–17, in the first sudden-death overtime championship.

Fads this year include go-karting and bowling.

▲ **JANUARY** Alaska becomes the 49th state in the U.S.

▲ **FEBRUARY** The world of rock 'n' roll is stunned by the news that Buddy Holly, Ritchie Valens and J.P. Richardson, Jr.—"the Big Bopper"—have all been killed in a plane crash near Mason City, Iowa. Fidel Castro becomes premier of Cuba.

▼ **MARCH** Mattel introduces Barbie. Hawaii becomes the 50th state.

MAY "Payola" scandals hit the news when radio disc jockeys admit to playing certain songs for cash.

▼ **OCTOBER** Wilt "the Stilt" Chamberlain makes his basketball debut with the Philadelphia Warriors.

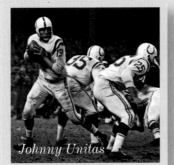

Johnny Unitas

Wilt Chamberlain

CHAPTER ONE

Kid stuff

Many toys became household names in the 1950s—the Hula-hoop, Frisbee and a perky blonde named Barbie. But nothing gunned Lynn Castle's engine like the small plastic cars sold at the local Pontiac dealership, DeWitt Barnette Motors, in his hometown of Boone, North Carolina.

"They cost $2 or $3 each," says Lynn, who still lives in Boone. "To earn money, I worked on my uncles' farms for 15 or 20 cents an hour. I didn't know anything about allowances from my parents, but my uncles would pay me to work.

"Whenever I had enough money, I'd go buy a car during one of our shopping trips into town," he continues. "Once my dad bought a light-green 1953 Chevrolet 210 Series car, and the salesman gave me a little plastic model just like it. I was thrilled to death."

Lynn still has more than a dozen vehicles, now worth hundreds of dollars apiece. "I'm tickled to death my parents saved them," he says. "I've never outgrown my love for those little cars."

Beloved toys weren't the only things that made growing up in the 1950s so memorable, as these next pages prove....

Chicago Child's Play

FOR THIS BUSY KID, THE SOUTH SHORE NEIGHBORHOOD HAD IT ALL.

By Jim Hemmen, Appleton, Wisconsin

My address from birth in 1939 until June 1955 was 7726 South Oglesby Avenue, Chicago, Illinois—in a neighborhood known as South Shore. I lived there with my dad, Mel, a pharmacist; my mom, Marilyn, a homemaker; and my sister, also named Marilyn.

My best friends were Tommy, Johnny and Ollie. Our playgrounds were vacant lots, alleys, houses under construction and the street.

Growing up in the 1950s, there was no Little League or other organized sports, but we rarely had trouble getting together a game. I remember Red Rover, kick the can, cowboys and Indians, cops and robbers and stoopball (bouncing a pink Hi-Flyer rubber ball off the front steps).

We also pitched pennies and played with marbles, Gilbert chemistry sets, Lincoln Logs and erector sets.

We got around on bicycles, wagons and roller skates that required a key to attach them to the soles of our shoes. We also made scooters from 2-by-4s with roller-skate wheels and push cars using wooden orange crates, curtain rods for axles and baby-buggy wheels or other wheels we found.

After my 10th birthday I joined the Boy Scouts. We had many campouts in the forest preserves in Chicago, hiked 20 miles on the Lincoln Trail in Springfield, attended summer camp at Camp West in the Owasippe campground near Whitehall, Michigan, and had Get Out the Vote campaigns and newspaper drives for recycling. During the summer of 1953, I went to the National »

Classicstock.com

Kid Stuff

Jamboree in California by train.

Saturdays were special. That's when I would go to the movie theater for newsreels, comedies and a double feature for 15 cents at the Shore on 75th Street, or 25 cents at the elegantly decorated Avalon on 79th and Stony Island. My favorite actors were John Wayne, Gene Autry and Roy Rogers.

Radio shows were also popular in our house. Many times we listened as a family, except to those that were made for children and were usually 15-minute serials. Among our favorites were *Boston Blackie, The Lone Ranger, The Shadow, Amos 'n' Andy, Burns & Allen, The Bob and Ray Show, The Jack Benny Program, Our Miss Brooks, Henry Aldrich, Suspense, Inner Sanctum, Fibber McGee and Molly, Let's Pretend, The Quiz Kids, Truth or Consequences, The Adventures of Superman, Batman* and *The Green Hornet.*

INTERPHOTO/Alamy

Our first TV was black and white with an 8-inch screen. The first program I can remember seeing was the coronation of Queen Elizabeth II in 1953. I also fondly remember *Hit Parade, Your Show of Shows* (with Sid Caesar and Imogene Coca) and *The Ed Sullivan Show.*

It wasn't always fun and games for young boys—we worked, too. I delivered the *Southeast Economist* and the *Chicago Daily News.* Most of my customers lived in three-story apartment buildings, so I would go up and down the alley and toss the papers onto their back porches. I had no such luck with the bulky Sunday editions. Later, I had a

Chicago Herald American paper route and delivered papers to about 100 addresses. One of my customers was Murray "The Camel" Humphrey, a Chicago gangster who gave me a $20 tip at Christmas.

I used the paper-route income to buy fireworks from a mail-order company. One year, we fired up one of our special rockets, and after it tipped over it set a garage on fire. We got in big trouble!

When I was 14, I got a job as a soda jerk in a drugstore. I learned to make malted milk, sodas and milk shakes. I served Green River and Cherry Coke beverages, as well as hand-packed ice cream and took deliveries. (I felt very important when I took prescription deliveries and less important when the delivery consisted of a pint of ice cream and a newspaper.) I also started working Saturdays in the drugstore and at shops in the Northwestern Railroad Terminal downtown.

Sure, I recall Wheaties, Rybutol vitamin tablets, Pepsodent toothpaste and '50s-era PF Flyers gym shoes—things people my age across the nation probably remember, too.

But I also have memories specific to Chicago, such as 10-cent hamburgers at White Castle, Bushman the gorilla at the Lincoln Park Zoo, the Currency Exchange where I got my Social Security card when I was 14, and bike hikes through Jackson Park to the Museum of Science and Industry—a wonderland for little boys like me.

My Chicago childhood holds memories that make me smile when I think about how wonderful it was to be a child of the '50s.

Photos, clockwise from top: Jim, second from left in front row, with Boy Scout Chicago Troop 595 in 1952; on his bike; second from right in front row with schoolmates; and holding a Christmas gift in 1953.

four legs and a tail

By Austin Killeen, Albuquerque, New Mexico

It was the fall of 1950 when my mother walked me down the steps to the basement of Woolworth's Department Store. For months, I had been badgering my parents for a dog, and today it appeared my dream

Tropical fish, turtles, parakeets and collies were some of the decade's most popular pets.

Classicstock.com

my **pets** *in the* **'50s**

journal entry

would come true. I didn't remember seeing any dogs at Woolworth's when my mother had taken me there before, but I certainly remembered a pet section.

Once downstairs, I eagerly turned in the direction of the pet department. Holding my hand, my mother led me to a gigantic glass tank full of water and little turtles. To my 8-year-old eyes, the tank looked like it could hold a battleship. Letting go of my hand, she asked, "What do you think?"

I knew what a turtle was but had never looked at one up close. The turtles seemed to swim frantically with their heads pushed up against the glass, as if trying to get to the other side. Suddenly, I was swept up with excitement at the thought of having one as my very own pet. When my mother asked if I'd like one, I excitedly replied, "Yes, yes, yes!"

As the saleslady tried in vain to scoop up one of the tiny little creatures, I asked, "What should I call it?" Having finally trapped one of the cute babies in her net, the clerk replied, "Myrtle would make a nice name." I liked the name.

When I left Woolworth's, I was as happy as any 8-year-old could be. It wasn't a dog, but it had four legs and a tail.

Sweet Dreams

The candy with the hole   only 5¢

the games we played

By John Hilpert, Louisburg, North Carolina

I'm often asked, "You're not from around here, are you?" My response is, "Nope, I was born and raised in Glendale, Queens, New York."

Many of the games we played in my old neighborhood were in the street, especially diamond ball, stickball and war. When the occasional car came, we would just stop and then re-start. Concrete sidewalks lined both sides of the street. Three-box baseball thrived here, along with jump rope, hopscotch and hide-and-seek. About half the houses were duplexes and the others single-family homes. A paved alleyway between the houses worked best for punchball and kings.

If a parent had ever tried to get involved with one of our games or even come to watch, we would have thought that terribly strange. It just didn't happen. Fathers worked away somewhere, and mothers kept to the house.

It's a wonder how all the rules for the games we played were passed down from one generation to another, since nothing was written down and there were no coaches. I remember that we younger kids would pester our older siblings' friends to let us play. Our pleas were almost always rejected. Then one day, they would be a player short, and our best player would be allowed to play. "Go way beyond the sewer hole and don't screw up!" they would tell us. Eventually, that 30-foot section of street became ours, and we drew on years of watching to know what to do.

We often played the same game for many days, until one day, we somehow magically knew it was time to do something different. "Choose up sides" gave each player an immediate value quicker than the stock exchange. No one ever had a uniform; we just showed up in jeans, T-shirt and sneakers. A key item in almost any street game was a "pinkie," a hollow-core pink rubber ball. If you were lucky and your mom bought you a Spalding, that automatically became the game ball. It cost more, but bounced true and lasted a long time. And in your pocket was almost always a piece of chalk to mark the bases with.

Secrets and strategies were of little value since sides changed each day, but competition was fierce. Yet as one game ended and the next began, the question of who had won and who had lost was usually forgotten. Bless children and their short memories.

Remember Saying?

kick

A fun or good thing

remembering a neighborhood

By Angie Eichhorn Klarke, Bluffton, Indiana

In the 1950s, my family and I lived in a post-World War II development in the small town of Decatur, Indiana. There were many young families on our block and we got to know almost all the neighbors.

As a child, I spent hours playing outdoors. The horseshoe-shaped street we lived on had very light traffic, which allowed my friends and me to use it as a playground. It was the ideal spot to jump rope, roller-skate, play kickball or hopscotch, and perform bicycle tricks.

In our front yard, we'd gather to play Red Rover, badminton and croquet and to run foot races. Sometimes, my friends and I just did "girl things" together, like playing Barbie dolls, practicing gymnastics and twirling batons.

One neighbor had the perfect tree for climbing. It was a birch that had stair-step-like branches that allowed us to climb up into the tree. There, we hammered an old board to use for a lookout bench, so we could spy on our neighbors.

POOL PALS. Author Angie Eichhorn Klarke, 3, with siblings Eileen, 4, and Dave, 2, cooling off in their front-yard pool in Decatur, Indiana in 1956.

Our neighborhood must have held fond memories for other kids, because some of them grew up and purchased homes on our street. I hope their children grow to have as many fun memories of Decatur as I do.

The author then (far left), the author now (left).

all ears

By Peggy Dudley
Aurora, Nebraska

From the first day that *The Mickey Mouse Club* appeared on television in 1955, I was hooked. I loved it!

I was 7, so my favorite Mouseketeers were Karen and Cubby—the ones closest to my age. As time went by, I grew to love them all, especially Annette, Darlene, Sharon, Doreen and Bobby. Those big-eared kids became as famous as Mickey Mouse himself.

When I watched the show, I made sure to wear my Mickey Mouse hat—a black felt beanie with round plastic ears. Even now, my dad chuckles at the memory of coming home from work at night and finding me engrossed in front of the TV, with my mouse ears firmly in place atop my head.

Each day's program had a theme. Monday was "Fun with Music Day," Tuesday was "Guest Star Day," Wednesday was "Anything Can Happen Day," Thursday was "Circus Day," and Friday, my favorite, was "Talent Roundup Day."

The music was wonderful, and I memorized the lyrics to every song.

Jiminy Cricket's song taught me how to spell "encyclopedia." And adult Mouse-keteer Jimmie Dodd strummed his guitar while offering commonsense advice, like practicing if we wanted to be good at something or listening to our teachers.

In addition to cartoons and other entertainment, the program also featured serials. My favorites were *The Adventures of Spin and Marty*, *Corky and White Shadow*, *Annette* and *The Hardy Boys*.

Spin and Marty was set on the Triple R Ranch, a boys' summer camp complete with horses, campfires and bunkhouses. Tim Considine and David Stollery played the title characters.

Tim Considine also appeared in *The Hardy Boys* with Tommy Kirk. Their characters, Frank and Joe Hardy, were amateur sleuths trying to help their father solve crimes.

Corky and White Shadow was a Western. Mouseketeer Darlene Gillespie starred as Corky, the spunky daughter of Sheriff Matt Brady.

Mouseketeer Annette Funicello starred in her own serial, *Annette*, about a country girl who moved to the city.

The Mickey Mouse Club holds a very special place in my heart. To this day, I still love M-I-C-K-E-Y —M-O-U-S-E.

RDA MKE

Bananas over Zip

By Janet Powers, Latham, New York

Summers in Yonkers, New York in the 1950s were great fun. Daily, my friends and I could be seen sitting on the steps of the local grocery store either reading Nancy Drew mysteries or playing with some of our toys. One of my favorite toys was Zip the monkey.

As a child, I loved monkeys. If I'd had my way, I would have had a real one as a pet. My parents wouldn't agree to that, but they did give me Zip.

He had a black plush body with a rubber face, ears and hands. He wore a yellow shirt with "ZIP" printed on the front, red corduroy pants with suspenders, a red hat and white rubber shoes.

Zip went almost everywhere with me. I couldn't take him to school, but he accompanied me on outings to the Bronx Zoo and Rockaway Beach. At Coney Island, he joined me on every ride, including the roller coaster. And I always took him with me to bed.

In 1963, we moved to Hastings-on-Hudson. I parted with many of my toys, including Zip.

A few years later, I married and moved to Latham, New York. I began to work and met a wonderful woman named Debbie Mahar, who introduced me to antique shopping and flea markets. I asked her if she ever found Zip the monkey on her antiquing jaunts, to please buy the toy for me.

Years passed, and one day I found a large box sitting on my desk at work. Afraid to open it, I looked through a crack in the box

MONKEY BUSINESS. Janet—and Zip—pose with Aunt Mary and Uncle Jerry Chorey in Atlantic City, New Jersey in 1954.

only to see Zip. My heart pounded and my eyes filled with tears as I recalled so many fond memories of my childhood.

Twenty years have gone by since Zip the monkey came back into my life. He sits on the bed in our spare room and is still as special to me today as he was when I was a small child. He's a constant reminder of treasured times past and my treasured friendship with Debbie.

Make Him the Happiest Boy in the World this Christmas...with

the Only Train   in the World with

MAGNE-TRACTION

THE NEW SENSATIONAL 1950

LIONEL TRAINS

Magne-Traction — exclusive Lionel track-gripping development — is the most amazing advance in model trains. More *speed*...top speed even around tight curves! More *climb*...up tough grades where other trains can't start! More *pull*...twice as many cars twice as fast! More *control*...split-second starts and stops. It's the grand climax to all the features that have made Lionel Trains the world's finest for 50 years...built-in remote-control whistle; real smoke (odorless, harmless); remote-control knuckle couplers; steel wheels, die-cast trucks. See these great Lionel Trains...*now priced lower than for many years past.* See Magne-Traction work! Free catalog at your dealer's or send coupon for special offer.

Look at the
**JOE DIMAGGIO
LIONEL CLUB HOUSE
TELEVISION SHOW**
EVERY SATURDAY
ON NBC NETWORK
See local newspapers
for time and station

*SPECIAL
COUPON
OFFER
ALL FOR 25¢*

LIONEL TRAINS, Post Office Box 446
Madison Square Station, New York 10, N. Y.
I enclose 25c. Please send me special Lionel Train Catalog offer postage prepaid.
1. The new Lionel 44-page full-color catalog.
2. The "Magic of Magne-Traction Book" with new track layouts, scenic effects, etc.
3. The Lionel "Portfolio of the 19th Century Locomotive Art Prints"—in color—suitable for framing.

Name...
Address..
City......................................Zone.........State.........

circa 1950

flavor of summer

My kids—Bill, 9, Butch, 6, Jo, 4, and Jean, 3—are as happy as they can be with watermelon on a hot summer day in '56.

— *Donna Warner*
St. Elmo, Illinois

Tune in to this prank

By Ken Cooke, *Gillett, Pennsylvania*

Sometime around 1955, when I was about 15 years old, Dad brought home our first television set. It was a Regal brand, and we got only one station.

Our house was built in the mid to early 1800s, and the bedrooms were upstairs. Built into the floor were old iron grates that you could open to get heat upstairs on cold winter nights. We could also open the grate in the front bedroom to observe what was going on in the living room below.

Remember the flat television wire that ran up to the big single-station antenna on the roof? Well, I got hold of about 20 feet of it and hooked one end up to the Philco radio in my bedroom. I ran the rest of the wire out the window, down the side of the house and into the living room, where I attached it to the TV.

Then I waited. That night, when Dad got comfortable in his old stuffed chair to watch the evening news, I turned up the volume on the radio—and the sound from my Philco came out of the TV. When Dad grudgingly got up to adjust the TV, I turned the volume on my radio down and, voila, the TV was "fixed"!

About the third time Dad got up to adjust the TV, I got to laughing so hard upstairs that he finally figured out something was up. He checked behind the TV and found the wire, which he promptly removed while muttering something about how those kids were going to ruin his TV. Dad was a man of few words, but that prank sure got him talking.

feed-sack fun

By J.R. "Dude" Hannon, Pelzer, South Carolina

As young boys growing up in the '50s in a small community on the outskirts of Pelzer in rural South Carolina, we had no television and very little in the form of entertainment. We had to invent our own games, such as "sack."

In town, there was a Purina Feed and Seed store that served the needs of the farmers. Owner George Poore provided free delivery and would travel the country in his old pickup, loaded to the brim with bags of feed. Sometimes, a bag would fall off and someone would find it and save it for Mr. Poore when he came through again.

To play the game, we would take an empty feed sack, fill it with straw, attach a long piece of twine to it and place it on the edge of the road after dark. We would choose a place with ample cover, so we wouldn't be seen. The "victim" would be driving along, see the bag, stop and get out of the vehicle to retrieve it. As he reached for it, we would take turns pulling it off into the bushes. Some of the folks would scream and others would say things that were not appropriate for young ears. It was great fun!

I'll never forget the night we played our last game of sack. Everything had been going well for us until people started to complain to our resident highway patrol officer, Tommy Huston. They said, "Some young 'uns are scaring the tarnation out of folks at night out there on Pelzer Road."

We were out that night in one of our best locations when Officer Huston rolled up in his patrol car with the car's right front wheel on our bag. As we tried to figure out what to do, he got out of the car with the red light flashing, then walked to the front of his car.

In the headlights' glare, we saw him pull the pistol from his belt. As he started to raise it into the air, we decided it was time to leave. As we made our move, we heard gunfire!

Everyone started hollering, and we knew we were getting hit while running through the nearby cornfield. I can still hear the sound of britches ripping on thorns and boys grunting as we ran for our lives.

The next day at school, we were pleased to discover that all of us had somehow come through the ordeal with only a few scrapes.

It was years later that I found out what really happened that night. Mr. Huston and my dad, James Jay Hannon, were close friends, and they cooked up a scheme to stop us from playing sack. That night as Tommy was getting out of his patrol car, my dad—unseen by any of us in the ditch—lit firecrackers with the pipe he always smoked. He told me he could hardly light more than one or two because he and Tommy were on the ground laughing so hard.

> *In the headlights' glare, we saw him pull the pistol from his belt.*

toy time!

POPULAR 1950s TOYS MORPHED INTO CULTURAL MAINSTAYS.

Some of the most memorable toys ever made hit the market in the 1950s, buoyed by a post-war consumer boom that gave marketers their first tantalizing glimpse of a consumption-minded colossus: the baby boomers.

While their prosperous parents snapped up color TVs and turquoise-blue appliances, youngsters clutching allowances turned toys like Frisbees and Hula-hoops into pop-culture icons. Another powerful duo fueled these toys' wild popularity: television advertising and Madison Avenue marketing firms, where men in gray-flannel suits convened over three-martini lunches, hatching plans to sell toys in unimaginable numbers. Boy, did they ever.

Here are some enduring favorites:

Barbie. Introduced in 1959, Barbie was both revered and reviled over the decades for her shapely hourglass figure. The brainchild of Mattel Inc. co-founder Ruth Handler, the 11-1/2-inch-tall plastic fashionista originally wore a black-and-white striped swimsuit, high-heeled shoes and gold hoop earrings. Named for Handler's daughter, Barbies first sold for $3 each; vintage, mint-condition, boxed Barbies now sell for thousands of dollars apiece. That'll buy a lot of zebra-striped swimsuits.

Pez. Austrian Eduard Haas II initially created Pez as a mint candy to help smokers kick the habit—hence the cigarette lighter-like dispenser. The name is derived from the German word for peppermint: **P**feff**E**rmin**Z**. In the early 1950s, the treat was introduced in the United States as a fruit-flavored candy, with dispensers topped with goofy, cartoonish heads. It was a smokin' hot idea; consumers still devour more than 3 *billion* candies annually, and vintage heads sell for thousands of dollars.

Silly Putty. In 1942, General Electric researcher James Wright tried to create a synthetic rubber. Instead, he developed a bouncy, pliable substance he called "nutty putty." Introduced as a novelty in 1950, it became a retail juggernaut, with more than 300 million units sold in plastic eggs. Who can forget squashing a handful of the gooey stuff onto a comic book page, peeling it off to reveal a perfect duplicate, then stretching it to distort the characters' faces? Big yucks, indeed.

Frisbee. Lovers of these fantastic plastic saucers can thank California carpenter Fred Morrison, who named his invention the Pluto Platter to capitalize on the 1950s UFO craze. The Wham-O toy company bought the product rights and introduced it as the Frisbee in 1957. Company execs came up with the name after hearing that Yale University students enjoyed playing catch with "Frisbies"—pie plates stamped with the name

Robin Beckham/Alamy

Photo Media/Classicstock.com

Classicstock.com

journal entry

Frisbie Baking Company, a local pie maker. They changed the spelling to avoid legal entanglements, and Frisbees have been flying high ever since.

Tonka Toys. Little boys bent on destruction met a formidable match in these virtually indestructible vehicles, originally built from automobile-gauge steel. Formally sold under the Tonka Toys name in 1955, the ubiquitous banana-yellow dump trucks, bulldozers and graders were more common in backyards than pink flamingos. The name Tonka (a Dakota-Sioux word that means "great") comes from Lake Minnetonka, which was visible from the company's first manufacturing facility in Minnesota. With more than 250 million sold, Tonka Toys are an American institution. Vroom vroom!

Hula-hoop. An epidemic of the hippy-hippy shakes hit America big-time in 1958, when the toy whizzes at Wham-O introduced brightly colored plastic Hula-hoops after learning that Australian children were gaga about shaking bamboo hoops around their hips. Popular? You bet, daddio. Consumers bought more than 100 million at $1.98 a pop during the first year alone. That's a whole lot of hooping it up.

my favorite '50s toys

in good humor

The Lang family was happy to see the Good Humor Man this August day in 1958 in Belmar, New Jersey. Neighborhood kids kept an ear out for the "ting-a-ling" so they could go get Mom and her purse.

— Edward Lang, Paramus, New Jersey

Remember Saying?

ankle-biter

A small child

Forever Hooked on Peter Pan

By Alice Schuler, Floral Park, New York

When I was 5 years old in the 1950s, three things happened to me: I was introduced to Peter Pan, I got the measles and I had my tonsils removed. I was confined to bed for about a week with each illness, which meant no television for me, since our only TV was in the living room.

At the time, I was enthralled with the whole story of Peter Pan. The book had been read to me numerous times, and I had seen the Disney cartoon and the Mary Martin special on TV. I also loved paper dolls—a perfect pastime when confined to bed. However, there were no commercial Peter Pan paper dolls available, or at least none that my parents could find.

So my father, who was a draftsman and a pretty fair artist, took on the project. He didn't just make me Peter Pan paper dolls, he drew large figures on heavy-duty cardboard and painted them with watercolors. All my favorites were there: Peter, Wendy, John, Michael, Tinker Bell, Captain Hook and Tiger Lily. He also made a pirate ship from a curtain-rod box and outfitted it with a sail and pirate flag.

I know I was the only child in my neighborhood to have such a wonderful toy, and I spent many happy hours in Neverland. I played with the ship and figures long after I recovered—so much so that my father made a second set after the first wore out. The second was colored with crayons—I helped with that.

Whenever I think of Peter Pan or being sick in bed, I think of those figures, the pirate ship, and all the love that my dad put into making them.

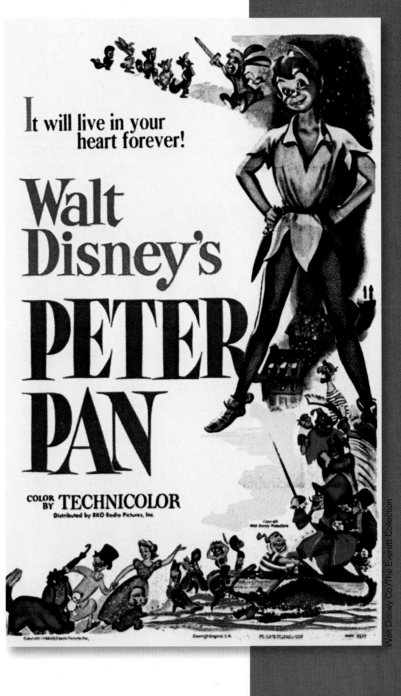

It will live in your heart forever!

Walt Disney's PETER PAN

COLOR BY TECHNICOLOR

Distributed by RKO Radio Pictures, Inc.

growing up in a flash

My husband, William, and I had so much fun with our two daughters, Tina and Patty, in the 1950s. We lived in Woodbury, New Jersey, and the girls just seemed to get more adorable with each passing year. From taking Patty to Brownies to playing dolls with Tina, those sure were good times!

— *Dorothy Tiver, Mantua, New Jersey*

From Playtime to Polio

By Trudy Taylor, Pollok, Texas

A child of the '50s, I moved with my family to Texas when I was 5. I was excited. That's where I believed Roy Rogers, my hero, lived.

It was good to be a kid back then. Every Saturday morning, we watched *Howdy Doody*. And each afternoon when we got home from school, we tuned in to *The Mickey Mouse Club*.

The neighborhood teemed with kids, who would gather almost every night to play all sorts of games like four square and hopscotch. We played outside until the streetlights came on.

But as wonderful as my childhood was, there were a few dark times that I'll never forget. One such scare was polio. Dr. Jonas Salk had just invented his vaccine and they started injections at my school in 1955. I remember taking a note home to get permission from my parents to receive the vaccine. I hated shots and was hoping they would decline the injection. No such luck.

It was hot the day my classmates and I were scheduled to get our shots. The teachers lined us up single-file and took us outside. When my turn came, the shot hurt like the very devil, but at least I didn't cry or get sick like some of the others.

Dr. Salk's vaccine changed the world, sparing many people from contracting that devastating disease. I feel lucky to have been a part of that wonderful time in history.

batboy was the best

By Richard McCabe, North Babylon, New York

Dad was a Yankees fan, so it was with reluctance that he took me to a New York Giants' game in the spring of 1951. Sure enough, I fell in love with the Giants.

I got a part-time job so I could save up carfare to take the "D" train to the Polo Grounds from our home in the Tremont section of the Bronx. Tickets weren't a problem—most of the gate personnel understood and let us in for free around the seventh inning.

Then one day in September 1953, I found myself in the right place at the right time.

I was waiting outside the stadium when a man came out of the Giants' clubhouse and asked me to get him a sandwich. When I returned, he offered me some money. I refused.

Four days later, the same thing happened. This time the man asked me if I wanted to work for the Giants. Of course, I said yes! He was Ed Logan, the Giants' clubhouse manager.

Early the next morning, Ed took me into the clubhouse and explained that the Reds were coming to town, and their equipment would be arriving soon.

I couldn't believe I was in the Giants' clubhouse. I walked over to Willie Mays' locker and touched his glove and uniform.

The Reds' equipment arrived, and Ed introduced me to "Little Pete"—the Yankees' assistant clubhouse manager.

As we were unloading the gear, I asked what my job would be. Pete looked at me with mock aggravation and said, "You're the batboy. Is that all right with you?"

For the rest of that season and the '54 and '55 seasons, I was the batboy for the visiting teams. I got to meet such great ball players as Roy Campanella, Stan Musial, Robin Roberts and Warren Spahn.

Before each game, I put the bats in their proper slots according to the batting order and got out towels and the water bucket. Once that was done, I could get my glove and join the players on the field during batting practice.

When the game started, I made sure there were two towels in the on-deck circle. I also brought out the weighted bat for practice swings and carried a pine-tar rag.

During the game, I retrieved the bats and shagged foul balls off the screen. When the visiting team was on the field, I sat in the dugout and watched the game.

It was a wonderful and exciting time. My friends also shared in my luck, as I usually had an armload of broken bats to take back to the kids in my neighborhood.

I feel privileged to have been a batboy at the Polo Grounds. And I'm still a Giants fan.

happy trails

Here's a picture of my wife, Cathy Tantillo, in 1951,
in front of her childhood home in Staten Island, New York.
She was 5 years old at the time and in love with Dale Evans
and Roy Rogers. She thought that if she dressed up like Dale,
just maybe she could appear on TV with Roy!

— *Charlie O'Brien, Niceville, Florida*

classic Rides

Red leather seats. White canvas top. A gleaming chrome grille. Whitewall tires. Bullet taillights. A 390-cubic-inch V8 engine. Rear seats with enough legroom for a dance floor. And glorious tail fins as tall as tomorrow.

No doubt about it: Few things looked finer prowling the streets of Whitefish Bay, Wisconsin than Chuck Hanson's flashy, fire-engine red 1959 Cadillac Eldorado convertible. It was one sweet machine.

"It was better than fabulous," Hanson says of his beloved Caddy, which featured an all-red interior and power everything. "I loved the tail fins. You could see 'em coming and going. I was 28 years old and paid about $5,800 for the car."

Good mileage? Fuggedaboutit. But who cared when gas cost a mere 30 cents a gallon?

After racking up 50,000 miles, Hanson traded in the Caddy for $75 in 1967. Today, the iconic auto fetches upwards of $100,000 in mint condition.

Nonetheless, he still owns priceless memories of his dream machine.

Cars were more than just vehicles in the 1950s. To understand why, read on....

No License...
No Problem

EXPERIENCED DRIVER AT 15 TOOK HIS FAMILY ACROSS THE COUNTRY

By Jim Sciortino, Trumbull, Connecticut

My 15th birthday— June 3, 1950— ushered in a summer of adventure that a teenager could normally only dream up. But for me and four other family members, the dream became a reality.

Image by Bob Heffley

Mom planned a 6-week cross-country trip from Bridgeport, Connecticut to California and back. Her goal was to visit relatives that neither she nor anyone else in our family had seen for the many years since they moved west.

I helped Mom and my cousin Virginia pack up our new 1950 Buick Special and settled my younger sister, Rosalea, and little brother, Carl, in the backseat. Then off we all went.

But as the saying goes, the best-laid plans of mice and men oft go astray—and so they did.

At our first gas stop, in New Jersey, as Mom got out of the car, a gust of wind flung the door in her face. The result was an instant migraine headache and blurred vision.

The gas station owner called for a local doctor, who forbade Mom from driving and suggested that we return home for her to rest. But Mom decided she could rest while

> *I asked her to pull over at a rest stop so I could take over the driving.*

Virginia drove the car.

Although Virginia had a license, she was not comfortable with her new responsibility or driving on unfamiliar roads.

After a few miles, I asked her to pull over at a rest stop so I could take over the driving.

My cousin was relieved, but my mom was upset about my driving without a license. I won the argument by reminding her that Dad had taught me to drive when I was just 12.

Dad was a family doctor who made house calls. Our phone would often ring in the wee hours of the morning, waking him for emergencies. Occasionally he would wake me to drive him on those calls because he feared he might fall asleep at the wheel.

Mom knew I was capable of driving, since I was already a seasoned operator at age 15. We agreed I would drive until Mom felt better.

That happened about 2 weeks into the trip, but, by that time, Mom was so comfortable with me driving while she or Virginia navigated that she let me continue.

Our route took us via southern roads and »

Author Jim Sciortino and his family took a 6-week ride across the country, stopping at Yosemite and the Grand Canyon.

In Pennsylvania, I drove past a speed trap and was stopped by the local sheriff.

highways to California, then followed a northern path back to Connecticut, over about 6 weeks. Zigzagging through 40 states, we stopped at as many national parks as we could and saw wondrous places like the Grand Canyon, Carlsbad Caverns, Yosemite, the Petrified Forest and the Great Salt Lake.

In California, my mom's cousin Dan arranged for us to watch part of the filming of *The Lemon Drop Kid*. Dan was a technical director at Paramount Studios.

We watched Bob Hope and Marilyn Maxwell perform on a soundstage and later met them and Ray Milland at the studio commissary. Dan must have been well liked because we were treated like royalty.

Our new Buick served us well—the only glitches being a flat tire in Wyoming and a broken set of ignition points in Chicago.

In Pennsylvania, I drove past a speed trap and was stopped by the local sheriff. He made my mom drive as we followed him back to the judge to pay a fine.

The judge was also the town barber, and his barbershop served as the courtroom. We had to wait for him to finish a haircut before he would see us.

When he was ready, the barber/judge opened a book of legal statutes and calmly said, "That will be $30 or 30 days."

I blurted out, "I'll take the 30 days. We can't afford $30!"

The barber/judge glared at me for a bit, then turned to the sheriff and said, "Get them out of here. I have no reciprocity with Connecticut, and I'm sure not going to feed this kid in our lockup."

I laughed about the barber/judge as we got under way, while Mom and Virginia sat in silent shock, finally bursting into giggles when we crossed the Connecticut border.

That summer of motoring across America is still one of my greatest adventures and among my fondest memories.

journal entry

my best motoring memory

"Let's get an economical car!"

"Right, let's get a DE SOTO"

It's hard to resist but easy to buy. It raises your

spirits but lowers your operating costs. It makes

driving a delight and shifting a memory.

Lets you drive without shifting!

Drive a De Soto before you decide!

De Soto-Plymouth Dealers present "IT PAYS TO BE IGNORANT" *starring Tom Howard every Wednesday night over CBS* · DE SOTO DIVISION, CHRYSLER CORPORATION

Saturday Evening Post, circa 1950

come and see the new cars!

By Frank A. Speney Jr., West Newton, Pennsylvania

I could hardly wait for the excitement of "new car announcement."

Back on February 17, 1958, my father, Frank A. Speney, opened the doors to his Chevrolet dealership in West Newton, Pennsylvania. Last year, Dad celebrated his 50th year with Chevrolet.

When the new models came out, car haulers would deliver the cars and trucks under wraps. This kept the public from seeing the body-style changes and all the new paint colors for the year. After the delivery was complete, the new cars and trucks would be washed, waxed and prepared for showing.

Local farmers waited to be called and asked to hide the new vehicles in their barns until it was time to display the new models in Dad's showroom.

> **Doors, hoods and trunk lids were opened and closed all day and night as the place buzzed.**

Before we knew it, the big 3-day event was upon us. Invited guests and curious car shoppers filled the showroom with their families in tow. Doors, hoods and trunk lids were opened and closed all day and night as the place buzzed.

The men were given yardsticks, pens, key chains and calendars. The ladies received perfume, rain bonnets, sewing kits and magnetic pot holders.

The children's eyes lit up at the balloons, coloring books and the cherry candy shaped like the Chevy bow-tie logo. Of course, everything had the address and phone number of the dealership on it.

There were tables filled with cookies—some purchased and lots homemade by customers using their favorite recipes.

Bakeries sent doughnuts and other treats with wishes for a prosperous year and hopes of attracting a few tire kickers to stop on the way home for a box of goodies. To wash down the baked goods, there was plenty of coffee, tea, hot chocolate and—yay—Nehi soda!

While viewing the autos over the years, customers were entertained by a three-piece combo band, an organist or even a squeezebox player playing "See the USA in your Chevrolet."

For Dad's 50th-anniversary event, flyers were sent to local newspapers and magazines, inviting customers old and new to a barbecue, tent sale and car show.

One of our old customers saw a flyer and called to tell us about Frank Flowers. When I called Mr. Flowers and explained who I was and why I was calling, I could hear the enthusiasm in his voice. We wanted to take pictures of his car—the first 1958 Chevy Impala convertible to come out of Dad's showroom!

While waiting for the photographer, Mr. Flowers told stories of parades, car shows and travels. He had everyone's attention. "Yep," he said, "it made it up Pikes Peak and back twice."

As I parked the car for the picture, I swear I could still sense that familiar new-car smell.

MEET YOUR
NEWEST CHEVROLET DEALER—

SPENEY CHEVROLET — YOUR NEW CHEVROLET DEALER
115 West Main St., West Newton, Pa.
Phone 77

FOLKS ! !

Summer will be here before you know it!

Chevy's Style inspired a whole new line of Women's Fashions . . . Chevy's value offers the lowest price of the low priced three, in the models most people buy! Speney Chevrolet is offering spectacular trades RIGHT NOW, during our April Sales Spectacular! You just can't afford to miss this 30-day Selling Spree . . . it's the biggest, most Spectacular Sales Celebration we've ever had! Come in today, and get our spectacular offer on the New Chevrolet Car or Truck that will get your job done faster, better and at lower cost per mile! TRADE NOW and SAVE . . . during the Gigantic April Sales Spectacular!

Your New Chevrolet Dealer . .

FRANK A. SPENEY, your newest Chevrolet dealer, is a veteran of the automobile business. Born and reared in McKeesport, Frank was associated with his father, owner of the Palace garage, for the last fifteen years. A Veteran of World War II, married and the father of three children, he is widely known in Western Pennsylvania automobile circles.

SPENEY CHEVROLET . 115 W. Main St., West Newton, Pa. . Phone 77

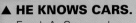

▲ **HE KNOWS CARS.**
Frank A. Speney has been selling Chevys for the last 50 years.

▲ **IN THE NEWS.**
Frank A. Speney announced the opening of his dealership in this ad that appeared in the local paper in 1958.

◄ **SHARING IDEAS.**
A quarterly business meeting with the western Pennsylvania Nash Auto dealers.

She's a Chevy Girl

By Eunice Jensen, Anoka, Minnesota

An afternoon in 1954 was about to get more interesting than the homework I was doing.

My folks had been picked up by some friends to go for a drive. I was finishing my math assignment. It was break time, and I went into the kitchen for a snack.

That's when the keys to my parents' car tempted me. They were where my dad always put them—on a little tray beside the stove.

Our car was in the driveway, but I knew I couldn't drive alone with only my temporary driver's permit. Still, I could practice backing down the length of the driveway a few times. Surely my folks wouldn't mind that.

All was going well until one of my friends came driving down the street as I was going up and down our driveway. He wanted to know what I was doing with "that hunk-of-junk Chevy."

I defended our '48 Chevrolet and said it was better than his Ford.

After a few more exchanges, I was challenged to a race to the end of the block.

I declined at first. But further insults from the Ford driver were too much for me.

We lined up in front of my house. Both cars had standard transmissions, but I was not intimidated.

The race took only a few seconds. I won! My friend drove away disgruntled, but the burden of guilt robbed me of any feeling of triumph. All I could think about was getting the car back into our driveway.

When I heard my folks come home, I was too shaken up to leave my bedroom.

Then the phone rang, and I heard my mother's end of the conversation: "When did this happen? I see. Thank you for calling."

My folks came into my room, and I knew it wasn't good. With a cool, controlled voice, my mother said, "That was our neighbor. I hear you took the car today and had a race down the street with some boy in another car."

Sobbing, I confessed it was all true.

Mother's answer was, "I hope you enjoyed yourself, because that is the end of any driving you will do." Then she left the room.

As I sat on the bed crying my heart out, my dad sat down beside me and put his arm around me. I told him that I felt so ashamed and wondered if they'd ever trust me again.

My dad consoled me and said, "Don't worry, honey. I know you learned a lesson. Mother will change her mind after a little while."

Finally, Daddy stood up and kissed me on the top of my head. As he was walking out, he turned and asked, "Who won the race?"

Even through tears, I managed a feeble smile and said, "I did."

Daddy said, "That's my girl," and left the room to smooth things out with Mother.

Eunice in 1956 and later posed with a '48 Chevy in 2009.

Jewels by Harry Winston

It Will Add to Your Happiness!

There is a great *plus* value that comes with a Cadillac which is very difficult for anyone to evaluate—except a Cadillac owner. To put it briefly, a Cadillac adds a goodly measure of happiness to a family's daily existence. It is not just the satisfaction which comes from fine performance and extraordinary comfort and out-standing safety and handling ease—thrilling though these things can be. It is more a sense of pride and family well-being—a joy of possession—and a consciousness of membership in the world's most distinguished group of motor car owners. Although difficult to explain and define—our owners can testify that it is very real and very valuable—a most moving reason for moving up to Cadillac. And remember —all this is in *addition* to the innumerable *practical* reasons for owning a Cadillac. It's too much to miss—any longer. We suggest that you come in and see us at your very earliest opportunity. We'll be delighted to see you at any time.

YOUR CADILLAC DEALER

circa 1953

look of success

When my husband got a new job with an insurance company in 1959 in Midland, Michigan, he was told he should look successful. So he bought new clothes and this baby-blue 1957 Chevrolet convertible our daughters Nancy and Debra are posing in. Wow! We really felt special driving that car around town.

—Lois Crites
Punta Gorda, Florida

the price to ride

COMPARED TO WHAT TODAY'S CARS COST, YOU COULD GET A NICE RIDE IN THE '50S FOR A REAL STEAL.

MODEL	1950	1959
Buick Roadmaster	$1,909	$3,856
Cadillac DeVille	$3,523	$5,252
Chevrolet Bel Air	$1,741	$2,386
Chrysler Windsor	$2,329	$3,204
Dodge Coronet	$1,927	$2,537
Ford Custom	$1,511	$2,219
Oldsmobile 88	$1,790	$2,837
Plymouth Deluxe	$1,492	$2,232
Pontiac Catalina	$2,000	$2,768
Studebaker Sedan	$1,565	$1,925

Bel Air was a beauty

By David Brondel, Centertown, Missouri

With only 3 short weeks left before facing the return to school in August of 1958, I'd normally have been depressed.

But back in July, Dad had ordered a brand-new Chevy from Bommel Brothers Chevrolet in Westphalia, Missouri. The delivery date was the first week of August, so Mom, my sister, Katy, and I waited eagerly for the announcement of our new arrival.

In 1958, anyone getting a new car was the envy of our small town of St. Martins. So Dad had a little spring in his step as he opened our front door after work. "Well," he said with a grin, "let's go get it!"

By the time Mom came out of the kitchen, Katy and I were already headed out the door toward our soon-to-be-traded '52 Chevy Deluxe.

The trip to Westphalia was like a trek to the moon. I counted every fence post and found 100 different positions a 10-year-old could assume in the backseat. When Dad announced that we were there, I left that Deluxe like it was on fire.

I raced to the building. "Dad," I yelled, "I can't find it. It's not here!"

"Just hold on, boy," Dad said with a bit of frustration. "We're not in the building yet. Keep your shirt on."

Once inside the showroom, a salesman shook Dad's hand and explained that the car was in the service area getting its final mechanical check.

Just when I thought my end was near, I heard the salesman tell Dad, "Well, let's go take a look, Mr. Brondel."

As we stepped through the doors to the service area, my eyes locked on the most beautiful car I'd ever seen. Two-tone paint, chrome trim and hubcaps accentuated the machine.

The colors—lavender and white—were new for 1958, we were told. (The car on *The Dinah Shore Chevy Show* was said to be this color, although there was no way to be sure on our black-and-white Philco television set.)

Katy was first to sit behind the wheel. She'd be 16 in 4 months and able to drive. I'd have to wait more than 5 years!

Then Dad got in, depressed the clutch and turned the key in the ignition, waking the 145-horsepower, 235-cubic-inch engine from its sleep.

Finally, I slid in behind the wheel, dreaming of the day I'd be able to operate this thing on my own.

That '58 Chevy saw me through my first date and a few more besides. It stayed in the family until '72, after the odometer had piled up 128,000 miles.

Dad's gone now, and so is that '58 Chevy. But my boyhood memories of a time when worries were few and summers were heaven will never fade.

DRAMATIC EDSEL STYLING leads the way
—in distinction, in beauty, in value!

Last August, the photograph above could not have been taken. The Edsel car was still a secret then. But in one short year, Edsel's outstanding design has become as familiar as it is distinctive. In fact, you can recognize the classic Edsel lines much faster, much farther away, than you can any other car in America! This extra value in advanced styling accounts for the many more Edsels you've been seeing on the road lately.

And proud new Edsel owners are getting plenty of extra value *inside* their cars, too—the ease of Teletouch Drive, the power and economy of the all-new engines, the convenience of self-adjusting brakes, the comfort of contour seats. And the satisfaction of having made a great buy. For there's less than fifty dollars difference between the magnificent Edsel and V-8's of the major low-priced makes.*

Why not see your Edsel Dealer this week for sure?

EDSEL DIVISION • FORD MOTOR COMPANY

Less than fifty dollars between Edsel and V-8's of the major low-priced makes

*Based on comparison of manufacturers' suggested retail delivered prices.

circa 1959

motor mouth

Any hot-rodder worth their chrome-plated grille knows that to be considered the king of the road, your street talk has to be up to snuff. Here's a lingo lesson for the rest of you squares.

Agitate the gravel: To leave.
Burn rubber or peel out: Leave tire marks.
Chariot: Car.
Deuce: 1932 Ford.
Flip-top: Convertible.
Go for pinks: Race for pink slip or ownership papers.
Floor it: Push the accelerator to the floor.

Hottie: Very fast car.
Jacked up: Describing a car with a raised rear end.
Ragtop: Convertible.
Stack up: Wreck a car.
Souped up: Modified for speed.
Tank: A large sedan.
Wail: Go fast.

Dad Came Home in a Frazer

By Judi Holdeman, Gold Hill, Oregon

My father purchased this kelly-green 1951 Frazer Manhattan new in New York City after returning to the U.S. for a 3-month leave from his job in Saudi Arabia. That's my mom next to the car on a second honeymoon at a redwood forest in northern California.

I remember how exciting it was for Dad to come home in this beautiful car after we hadn't seen him for so long. I was 11 years old, and it seemed like he had been gone forever. He arrived home on Father's Day, and I had embroidered a handkerchief for him as a gift.

Dad was quite the comedian. When we'd take drives into the country with the Frazer and we'd smell a skunk, he'd make us laugh at the smell. To this day, when I smell a skunk, I get a good feeling recalling the wonderful times we had.

no rest for the weary

By Lillian Claunch, Des Moines, Washington

In the summer of 1950, after 4 years of medical school and 1 year as an intern—with me working outside the home to keep the financial ship afloat—my husband, Joe, and I were ready to meet the world.

Now, where to start a general practice? One ad featuring South Bend, Washington intrigued us. Checking a map, we saw it was about as far away from Columbus, Ohio as one could get.

The ad was for a partnership with a doctor in an established general practice. A telephone exchange with Dr. Profitt of South Bend confirmed our intention.

We would have to drive across the country on a shoestring—and a pretty threadbare one at that.

Joe's bright idea of replacing our old Mercury's front seats with used Nash seats worked almost perfectly. They were a fraction too wide, but we just had to slam the doors hard to latch them. The Nash seats folded down flat! There was our bed.

We headed northwest and made more than 500 miles the first day. As night approached, we looked for an out-of-the-way country road where we could sleep.

Then, along a river, we found the perfect place—a quiet country lane with a tree-lined turnout. We gratefully parked, put down our seats and conked out.

Not long after that, all hell broke loose. An unmuffled engine blasted our ears zooming past us, and an angrier one followed.

Just as the sound of those engines was fading, a herd of motorcycles roared in pursuit. It sounded like the race was coming right through our open window. Then came the sirens! We laughed hysterically.

The next day, we barely made Iowa. Tired as we were, we spent another night on our Nash-seats bed—a quiet one this time.

The following night, we decided to treat ourselves to a motel room. We turned off Route 10 and into a small town, looking for a cheap place to stay. A motel sign offered us a soft bed and a hot shower for only $6.50.

In the middle of the night, a freight train seemed to tear right through our room. It rattled the bed and shook the shaving cream off the sink.

Now we knew why the motel was so cheap. Railroad tracks right behind a motel? We couldn't stop laughing.

Fortunately, no more drag races or trains plagued us the rest of the way to South Bend, a small town of about 9,000.

It took us 5 adventurous days and sometimes raucous nights to get there, but we received a warm welcome and promptly fell in love with the Pacific Northwest, where we lived together for more than 40 years.

an easy fix

By Fred Di Francesco, Melbourne, Florida

A few months after I'd been discharged from the Army, I bought a new 1957 Chevy Bel Air in Philadelphia. My mom cashed in a $500 insurance policy she had on me when I turned 20, and I used that money for the down payment.

I had the car about 3 years when it started stalling occasionally. After getting it towed to a service station, the mechanic would look around, pull on the spark plug wires and say, "Try it now." Sure enough, the car would start, but we didn't know exactly what the problem was.

The last time it happened, I had it looked at by my buddy's 80-year-old father, who owned an inspection station. He found the problem right away. The coil was installed upside-down, and with oil all over it, the distributor wire kept falling out.

Every time a mechanic checked the spark plug wires, he would put the coil back, too, not knowing it had come off on its own.

My buddy's dad put a whole roll of electrical tape around the coil to hold it in place, and it lasted 2 more years with absolutely no trouble.

Classic Rides

Nash had a bad reputation

By George Wilberg, Salamanca, New York

Having driven clunkers for years, my father, Edward Wilberg, hankered for his first brand-new car.

Working at a GE refrigerator plant full time in Erie, Pennsylvania and earning money from his grape farm, Pa finally saved up enough money to realize his dream and snapped up a classic gray 1951 Nash Statesman Airflyte.

This was a distinctive car of its day, having at least 20 percent less drag due to its "upside-down bathtub" appearance. It also had a one-piece windshield—which was way ahead of the "big three" automakers—and good gas mileage of 27 miles per gallon.

A special feature was a split-back front bench seat, with both halves able to recline to form a double bed. That item got the family in trouble one night.

My parents and their three sons—Edward, Peter and me—all were excited about a night at the drive-in movie theater. But we were not allowed in! The reason was a ban on Nash vehicles with the reclining seats, known as great make-out cars.

My dad's protest that he was a married man with three sons along didn't help. After much debate, however, families were finally able to bring such cars to drive-ins without a hassle.

We affectionately called the car "the gray whale" for its bulbous shape. My father complained that it took half of Texas to turn the Nash around, due to its closed-in front fenders. But a 20.4-gallon tank allowed us to drive all the way to New York City without stopping for gas.

journal entry

my favorite wheels

Leading designers
agree that
THE FLIGHT-SWEEP
is the car style trend
of the future!

PLYMOUTH BELVEDERE 4-DOOR SPORT SEDAN HARDTOP

"This is the direction all car design should ultimately go."
Ted Jones, *boat designer, Slo-Mo-Shun, Miss Thriftway and "X-100"*

"The Flight-Sweep is the freshest approach yet in the evolution of car design."
Edward F. Burton, *Chief Engineer, Douglas DC-8 Jet Transport*

"The Flight-Sweep looks like motion. It's eager, vital with a feeling of the future."
Anne Fogarty, *fashion designer*

All over America there is increasing acceptance of THE FLIGHT-SWEEP, the exclusive design of the 1956 cars of Chrysler Corporation. People agree that the long, low aerodynamic lines from headlight to upswept tail make this design that others must follow in the years to come.

Leading designers in many fields, such as those above, back up this judgment. These experts find THE FLIGHT-SWEEP appealing in its expression of modern living . . . youthful, dynamic.

And it has a generous touch of the future!

See and drive the 1956 Plymouth, Dodge, De Soto, Chrysler or Imperial. No other cars offer so much in style, in driving ease, in performance, in *value* . . . and offer it to you *first!*

CHRYSLER CORPORATION ➤ THE *FORWARD* LOOK
PLYMOUTH · DODGE · DE SOTO · CHRYSLER · IMPERIAL

Saturday Evening Post, circa 1956

Semper Fi, Girls!

By DeWayne Johnston, Butler, Pennsylvania

In 1958 Butler, Pennsylvania, a high school boy who couldn't make an impression any other way could at least do it with a nice car.

Neither my buddy Newton Tack nor I could afford our own cars, so we had to make do with a 1956 Buick, owned by Newt's father.

Our luck changed when Newt's older brother, Jack, went into the Marine Corps and entrusted Newt with his car.

Jack had graduated and saved enough money for a '57 Chevy Bel Air two-door hardtop. It was red and white with a continental kit and a 283-cubic-inch, power-pack engine.

Our status improved at the local hangout, Morgan's Wonder Boy Drive-In restaurant. Girls would talk to us, some even agreed to go for a ride.

The Chevy's windshield sported a Camp Lejeune parking sticker, and the continental cover in back had "USMC" on it. The Marines connection was obvious but, as usually happens, overconfidence leads to a fall.

To girls we didn't know, we would bluff that we were Marines on leave. That made an impression…except for the night a carload of real Marines pulled in beside us and started asking questions we couldn't answer.

Another show-off stunt was to race other guys over the hill on Main Street. The '57 was fast and didn't lose very often.

But Newt had a habit of holding the automatic transmission in the passing gear many RPMs past the shift point.

By the time we got to the top of Main Street, smoke was rolling out from under the '57 as the transmission let go. We coasted into the lot beside the drive-in, shrouded in embarrassment, and called a tow truck.

Newt paid for the transmission repair and didn't tell his brother until much later. But our show-off days were over.

from cool wheels to hot rods

These boss add-ons worked wonders in transforming even a ho-hum set of wheels into the ultimate '50s dream machine.

* Custom paint job
* Fender skirts
* Dashboard hula girl
* Coon tail for antenna
* Rubber shrunken head
* Tuck-and-roll upholstery
* Lake pipes

* Fuzzy dice
* Continental spare cover
* Curb feelers
* Suicide steering knobs
* White sidewall tires
* Skull shift knobs

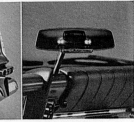

JUST LOOK AT THE PLYMOUTH FEATURES THE OTHER LOW-PRICE CARS DON'T HAVE...YET!

SWIVEL FRONT SEATS (standard on Sport Fury models) make getting in and out easier. A wide armrest pulls down between the seats when two ride in front instead of three.

PUSH-BUTTON CONTROL CENTER groups instruments in plain sight, controls in easy reach. Pushbuttons on left control automatic shift*. On right of the wheel: Push-Button Heater and Defroster*.

REAR SPORT DECK (standard on Sport Fury models) is one of the many features that give the low-price '59 Plymouth such a high-price appearance. No other car looks so refreshingly youthful — nor runs so nimbly!

MIRROR-MATIC rear-view mirror* eases tensions of night-time driving by electronically dimming the glare from headlights of the cars behind you.

These are only a few of the many new convenience, safety and performance features you'll find on the '59 Plymouth. Don't look for them on any other low-price car . . . *only Plymouth offers them*. Before you buy *any* '59 car, see Plymouth. It's exactly what you've always wanted! Let your Plymouth dealer prove it—soon.

* optional at low extra cost.

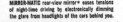

Plymouth
today's best buy, tomorrow's best trade

circa 1959

A Man and his Packard

By Bill Larmore, Marietta, Georgia

Many people likely remember the wonderful Packard and its slogan, "Ask the man who owns one!"

Just before a Packard came into our family, our 1946 Chevrolet sedan was sounding like a junk grinder. My daily trips from our Atlanta home to my job at Lockheed in Marietta, Georgia had become about as relaxing as snake-handling.

One Saturday morning, in July of 1955, I was changing generator brushes on the Chevy only to note that the fuel pump was leaking. I stalked into the house and informed my wife, Eloise, that I was going downtown to look for another car.

"Just go ahead!" she replied. "When you get back, you can park the new car and come in to help me figure out the down payment on braces for Cathy's teeth!"

I strode out of the house and made my way to Atlanta's automobile row. I noted "Packard"

carved in stone over a huge doorway on Spring Street. I went in as if mesmerized.

I found that the remaining staff at Atlanta Packard Motors was finishing the sad job of closing out all remaining stock before closing the doors for good.

I found myself looking at the most beautiful mechanical monster I had ever seen—a 1951 like-new Packard four-door with only 24,000 miles on it. The giveaway price, as I recall it, was $500 plus my wreck.

I gave the salesman 10 bucks to hold it and herded my poor Chevy home, where I rushed in with the great news. Eloise, busy wiping little noses and bottoms, took the news with less than frenzied excitement.

"Bill," she said, "if you and Lockheed can pay for that rich man's car on a poor man's salary, then go ahead. But you are going to have to take out a credit-union loan to get it, and the minute you take food out of our children's mouths to keep it, it's gone."

Suffice it to say that all members of my family remained well fed. The Packard served as our loyal and highly trusted family car for more than 14 years before being retired from everyday use.

Folks who change their cars whenever the tire tread gets thin will be surprised to know that I'm still enjoying that huge, purring black Packard.

You can ask the man who owns one.

fill 'er up, please

Remember when gas stations were called
service stations because you got real service?
Claude Burnett of Columbia, South Carolina, who shares
this photo, does. That's his 1953 Chevrolet Bel Air at a
Pure Oil station in Williamston, North Carolina in '54.
Two attendants were on hand, and there were tires and other
automotive items for sale, plus two service bays. Today,
you pump your own gas, check your own oil and wash your
own windows. You might even be charged for air!

Family times

Times were as lean as chicken broth on the farm where Sandy Owens grew up during the 1950s in Cushing, Oklahoma.

"Sometimes the only food came from Dad's hunting," recalls Sandy, now of Montague, Texas. "But we never wanted for anything.

"We played outside a lot. We roller-skated, made mud pies, chased horny toads and caught lightning bugs, which we'd put in mason jars to make our own little night lights."

The annual family vacation was a camping trip to Lake Texoma for swimming, fishing and exploring. At night, Sandy relished the starry view—from a mattress in the bed of a pickup truck.

Memorial Days also were memorable. An army of her mother's relatives would go to the cemetery to place flowers on family graves, then share a potluck dinner.

"It was one of the only days we were allowed to drink soda," Owens says. "I still remember the taste of grape Nehi soda."

Lean times? Sure. But family provided a wealth of comfort and security.

Read on for more about the ties that bind....

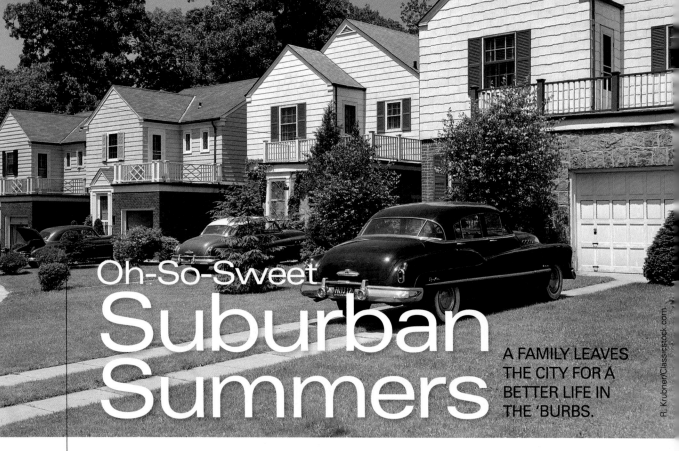

Oh-So-Sweet
Suburban
Summers

A FAMILY LEAVES THE CITY FOR A BETTER LIFE IN THE 'BURBS.

By Janet Apuzzo, Trumbull, Connecticut

I grew up on Long Island, New York in the 1950s along with about a gazillion other kids whose dads served in World War II. A veteran could buy a house with no down payment as long as he could afford the mortgage. Tract developments originated by William Levitt (of Levittown fame) began popping up all over the flat, once-potato-farmed landscape. Multitudes of young families joined the exodus out of the ethnic cocoons of New York City into this new heterogeneous mix of suburban vets' families.

We moved to our split-level in Plainview in the spring of 1955. It cost a hefty $15,000. My grandmother in the Bronx cried as if we were leaving the planet. And it really was another world. The houses, one after another, were lined up on the street with a neat little patch of dirt in front and a small backyard. Every evening after work, all the dads were out there watering the freshly seeded dirt to make the grass grow. And grow it did. I remember waking Saturday mornings to the sweet smell of cut grass amid the cacophony of all the lawnmowers on the block buzzing away.

Living the Good Life

Life couldn't have been better. Even Dad, who had to drive to Manhattan every day in a suit and tie in our Ford station wagon without air conditioning, loved it. He felt proud to be the master of such a "rich man's house," as our grandma called it. He'd return from work after 2 hours in traffic, and we'd have to quit playing ball to come home to kiss him as a sign of affection for his efforts.

There were so many kids in our neighborhood that we practically lived outdoors. We would choke down our supper to get back outside in time to get on the good team for the after-dinner game. Some summer nights, when the parents sat out in the backyard instead of the front, we got the chance to play the forbidden game of "you »

For families like Janet Apuzzo's, life in suburbia was an absolute dream come true. These snapshots show Janet with her parents, younger sister and toy dolls around the mid-1950s.

can't run me over." It was a game best played when it was getting dark.

The kids on the block would sit on the curb with their feet in the street and their eyes closed. We would chant the name of the game tauntingly and incessantly, and whoever had their bikes with them would ride really close to the curb. The object was to flip yourself back and lift your legs quick so your feet didn't get run over! I was a real daredevil and waited until the last second before flipping back. It was heart-stopping, mad-screaming fun!

Family Fun

The best part of the summer was Dad's vacation week. We ate out every night so Mother didn't have to cook. "It's your mother's vacation, too," Dad would say, and Mother would bask in the luxury of it. We went to Jones Beach a lot that week—with sandwiches and fruit stuffed into the 2-ton metal cooler that Dad would hoist up on his big shoulder and grunt and sweat as he carried it through the parking lot onto the beach. One of the middle kids carried the thermos of Kool-Aid and was always told to be careful not to drop it because it had glass inside. And the big kids carried the chairs for the grown-ups. Dad would make a second trip to the car for the wooden playpen for the baby.

Also on Dad's vacation, we went to Jolly Roger, which had amusement rides, and—best of all—a carousel. If you were big, you could ride the horses that went up and down on the outer perimeter. There was a figurine you passed on the way around that dispensed rings. You could stand up on the stirrups of your horse and try to grab a ring as you went by. It wasn't easy. You had to hold that horse with one hand and lean way

In those days, we walked everywhere we wanted to go...and I mean miles!

out at the same time with the other. There was a rumor that there were gold rings, but I never grabbed any except silver. It didn't matter, though; it was joy beyond reason.

On the Go

In those days, we walked everywhere we wanted to go…and I mean miles! We walked to and from school during the week, and on Saturday afternoons, we walked to confession by order of the Holy Father (mine). If you wanted to join Girl Scouts, you had to be able to walk there and back. Or we rode our bikes—to the dentist, to piano lessons, to the candy store, to the doctor to get a wart removed. If you couldn't get yourself there and back, you weren't allowed to go. (Mother was just too busy cleaning the house to drive us.)

Life was simple and innocent then: eating watermelon in the summer, wearing baby-doll pajamas on a hot night with the fan blowing in my bedroom, dressing my perfect Barbie and Ken, doing the cha-cha. Oh, I miss those days. It's too bad we get to live them only once.

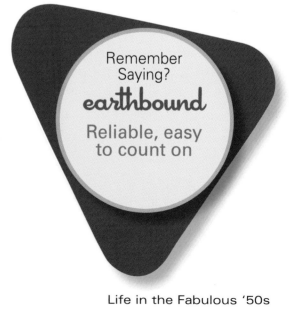

Remember Saying?

earthbound

Reliable, easy to count on

The SARATOGA—4-Bedroom Ranch Type

Choose YOUR *New Home*

from dozens of lovely
new NATIONAL designs

Large house or small house—whichever you need; Ranch-type, Cape Cod, Traditional—whichever you prefer. National offers virtually unlimited variety in two, three and four bedroom homes, some with two baths, also porches, breezeways, garages, and fireplaces. Save hundreds of dollars. Save months of waiting. Get a *National* Home!

ASK YOUR LOCAL NATIONAL HOMES DEALER for details — or send 25¢ for new edition of "Your National Home Magazine," big 64-page book of pictures, plans, home-owning facts. Address National Homes Corp., Dept. HH7, Lafayette, Indiana.

National Homes prefabricated panels and structural parts are commended by Parents' Magazine as advertised therein.

CORPORATION, Lafayette, Ind.
EASTERN PLANT: HORSEHEADS, NEW YORK

Household, circa 1952

Price of the Good Life

Back here at home, amid concerns of the Korean War, young couples continued their migration to new homes. Many of these houses were prefabricated and located in outlying areas of their communities. This lifestyle added a new word to the nation's vocabulary— "suburbia."

The typical suburban house was ranch-style, generally with two bedrooms and an attic that could be converted to two more bedrooms and a bath. Prices ranged from about $8,000 to $11,500— with major appliances usually included.

Those prices were typical on the East Coast. On the West Coast—in Seattle, for example—you could buy a home built of masonry block for $4,999, including the lot.

In most areas of the country, you could get a government-guaranteed mortgage for a 5 percent down payment (veterans didn't have to put anything down), with 30 years to pay. The monthly payment came to about $56.

To furnish that home, you needed to budget your money so you could buy big-ticket items—such as a two-piece living room suite for $157, a seven-piece dining room set for $149 or a three-piece bedroom set for $139!

Classicstock.com

in the '50s, I remember...

...no air conditioning, but it was perfectly safe
to leave the windows open at night;
...paying bills in person every week;
...going to the meat market, then to the greengrocer;
...milk, coffee and tea delivered right to your door;
...one-car families;
...going barefoot all summer;
...eating at the local burger joint (before fast food);
...and getting home late from the movies.
Our parents only worried about what trouble we might
get into—not what might happen to us.
All in all, the 1950s were a better time to live...and grow up!

— *Frank Roberts, Gainesville, Georgia*

curb service

By Marilyn Stone, Columbus, Ohio

I wonder: How many people have actually seen a shoemobile?

When we moved into our house in 1959, we were the first family on our street in a new neighborhood in Columbus, Ohio.

Because the wives in one-car families could become isolated, there were many services that came to your door, including the infamous Shoemobile.

The man driving the shoe-repair truck would fix your shoes on the spot. Another company bronzed baby shoes.

Of course, the Welcome Wagon service was there to provide us with goods, and we had the usual door-to-door arrivals of the Fuller Brush man and salespeople from carpet and drapery companies, insurance agencies and vacuum-cleaner companies like Electrolux, Kirby and Rainbow.

We'd also get occasional visits from a photographer with a pony for the kids to pose with.

You could count on some services like clockwork. Mail was delivered twice a day—at 10:30 a.m. and 2:30 p.m.—and the mailman carried stamps to buy.

We'd get an ice-cream truck twice a day, and on Saturday nights a truck would come around with its bell ringing and we'd all rush out for doughnuts made right there.

The Omar Bakery man showed up Mondays, Wednesdays and Fridays, the egg man was there once a week, the vegetable man showed his produce on Thursdays and the Charles Chips salesman sold potato chips in big tin cans.

Diaper service was available at your door, as was TV repair, dry cleaning, and grocery and drugstore delivery.

You could even have shrubbery landscapers draw up

plans right on the spot, and doctors made house calls. About the only services we didn't have close by were dentists and schools, although that lasted only a couple of years.

There also wasn't any garbage collection, so we had to burn everything in a steel drum in the backyard.

Like a few other housewives, I didn't drive back then, and my husband was usually driving our car either to his job at Freiden Calculator or to school.

So I was glad to have all the service people back then. I'm still living in the same home—and I miss them all.

best foot forward

Here's a wonderful picture of my mother, Elizabeth O'Neil Glockner, in 1957. She is polishing shoes for six of her children, ages 4½ months to 6 years, in this photo before getting them ready for Sunday church on Mother's Day.

Mom and Dad ended up having a total of 12 children! Luckily for the family, Mom was a home-economics major and could stretch a dollar a mile while sewing all our clothes, quilting and keeping an organized, loving home. We grew up in the country on the outskirts of Portsmouth, Ohio and have the best memories ever.

— *Colleen J. Isaacs, Cuyahoga Falls, Ohio*

The Everett Collection

Doo-Wop Lullaby

By Karen DeVilling Mulhollem, Ocala, Florida

Music was a big part of my childhood in Pittsburgh, Pennsylvania during the '50s. I remember visiting my grandmother and going to sleep with the window open, listening to the doo-wop sounds coming from the corner where musicians honed their skills.

My father had a side job as a professional guitar player. Every Saturday night that someone had a get-together, the band my dad belonged to played all the '40s songs my parents and their friends remembered from the war days. The band also performed the day's popular songs. Dad had a beautiful guitar solo in *Perfidia*. And I fell asleep on my mother's lap many times to country-western songs, such as *Tumbling Tumbleweeds*, and Hawaiian music like *My Little Grass Shack*.

I was the best of friends with the little sister of a member of a rock 'n' roll group called the Dell Vikings. We used to slip in and sit on the stairs to the basement where the members practiced. Who knew they would be famous within a few years? *Come Go with Me* was one of their songs—and my favorite. It still is.

grand days with my grandparents

By Frances D.A. Woytowich, Honesdale, Pennsylvania

Life was certainly simpler in the 1950s—especially at Grandpa and Grandma's house.

I was 5 years old in 1955, living in Sussex, New Jersey. My grandparents had a huge garden back then, where they grew peas, lima beans, marrowfat beans, spinach, tomatoes, strawberries and melons. They also had several fruit trees. We enjoyed our share of fresh-plucked peaches, apples and cherries.

Grandpa also tended a butternut and hickory-nut tree. Grandma would add the rich, flavorful nuts to her home-baked cakes and cookies. Every time we visited, Grandma had some kind of dessert waiting, or a candy jar full of gumdrops. Not to be outdone, Grandpa would make his delicious oyster stew. No one went hungry in their home.

Besides baked goods, Grandma made her own soap—for dishes, laundry and bathing. She would also braid rugs with pieces of rags. Looking back, she spent a lot of time at the sewing machine.

On holidays, the entire family would gather at Grandpa and Grandma's for a feast fit for a king. You could always count on leftovers, but could only enjoy them after the dishes were done!

We belonged to the Sussex Methodist Church, which was founded by my grandparents. We attended every Sunday, going to both Sunday school and worship. Afterwards, we would visit the local ice-cream shop for homemade ice cream and pie. When we returned to the house, Grandma would set me on her lap in the rocking chair and sing:

> "Won't you come over to my house?
> Won't you come over and play?
> I've lots of playthings, a dolly or two
> We live in the house 'cross the way,
> I'll give you candy and sweet things,
> I'll put your hair in a curl,
> Won't you come over to my house?
> And play that you're my little girl."

Yes, it's true that in those days, we didn't have much money. But who needed money when life with Grandma and Grandpa was so rich?

D. Corson/ClassicStock.com

Remember Saying?

circled

Married or engaged

65

a home of our own

By Madeline Huss, Bowie, Maryland

"Anyone who buys a house 30 miles from the city is out of his mind!"

I'll never forget when my father-in-law made this statement, because that's just what my husband, George, and I were about to do.

It was 1956, and tract homes were springing up all over New Jersey. They were for people like us—couples with kids, not much money and a longing for a place of our own.

The '50s were a time of great change, with moving vans crossing the country as veterans of World War II and Korea looked for affordable homes.

We lived on the third floor of an ancient building on the outskirts of Newark. We'd been thrilled to get this rent-controlled apartment within walking distance of Branchbrook Park.

After our second child was born, though, the charm of that apartment was gone. It was 19 steps up to the terrace, eight to the entrance, then two more flights to our door.

It was work enough with a toddler and the baby, but grocery day meant several trips down to the car.

"That's it," George said one day after a shopping trip. "We're going to buy a house."

I shrugged. "That's easy to say…but how can we afford a house when we can barely scrape up rent each month?"

We scoured the countryside every weekend and finally found a modest development of Cape Cods and ranch houses in the town of Old Bridge. There, for only $250 down, we could purchase a brand-new, two-bedroom home.

When moving day arrived, I did have second thoughts. From our apartment, the grocery store and library were only two blocks away…but in our new place, the nearest A&P was 9 miles off!

In our old neighborhood, huge oak trees shaded our street. In our new one, the twigs planted in front of our model home wouldn't provide shade until our 30-year mortgage was paid off.

However, I soon discovered that our new home was in a real neighborhood—and the clothesline was a wonderful place to meet neighbors. As we pinned up diapers and underwear, we exchanged our vital statistics— little money, many children, one car.

It didn't matter how many cars we had, since none of us women could drive, anyway. We were marooned amid the mud and crabgrass!

> *I discovered that our new home was in a real neighborhood—and the clothesline was a wonderful place to meet neighbors.*

my memories of home

Another gathering place was the septic tank. Someone's was always overflowing, so the men of the neighborhood would pitch in on Saturday for a communal septic tank repair. That night, the family with the bad septic tank usually hosted an impromptu party.

We didn't need nursery schools or day care. The little-traveled street served as a giant playground, and the milkman and bread man knew to wend their way carefully through the maze of children.

We lived there for 10 years and still go back to visit. The trees have grown and most houses now have two cars parked out front.

To an outsider, we didn't have much going for us in the '50s—just a lot of hard work, a lack of luxuries and lots of kids to take care of. Yet, looking back, I can tell you that we enjoyed every minute.

little slugger

Here's my son Mike, then 8 months, in '55 exploring the contents of my kitchen cabinets. Always on the lookout for pots to bang with a wooden spoon, he's ready for action in his handmade Yankees uniform.

— *Lucille Duh*
Piscataway, New Jersey

Bellybands for Baby

By Eileene Walton, Dennison, Ohio

In 1951, I was "in the family way," as it was called back then. The months before the baby's birth were some of the most exciting. That's when you'd prepare for the arrival of your little blessing, and getting ready was definitely part of the fun!

My husband and I didn't go out and buy a lot of furniture or other items for the baby. In fact, I made my own diapers and gowns. I would embroider the gowns and crochet ties along the edges.

My husband was a clay worker and made 37 cents an hour, so we could afford just a little something for the baby each payday. Today, no one uses bellybands, but at the time, a baby needed six to eight of them. So on paydays, I got to buy one for 15 cents.

When the baby was born, you placed a silver dollar enclosed in fabric over the baby's navel and covered it with a bellyband to hold it in place. This was to ensure a nice flat "in" belly button and help support the baby's back!

©iStockphoto.com/SweetyMommy

Classicstock.com

STATEMENT

KENOSHA HOSPITAL ASSOCIATION

6308 EIGHTH AVENUE — KENOSHA, WISCONSIN

Date 10/30/50 195_

Mrs. June Nelson & Baby
4805 - 5th Avenue
Kenosha, Wisconsin

ALL BILLS ARE PAYABLE AS ISSUED

BALANCE—Account Rendered

Nursing Service, Board and Room				
From 10/22	To 10/29 (7)	at $ 7.00 Per Day		49.00
From	To	at $	Per Day	
From	To	at $	Per Day	
Infant Care	6 days	at $ 2.50 Per Day		15.00
Operating Room or Delivery Room				10.00
Anesthesia				5.00
X-ray				
Laboratory				5.00
Drugs and Dressings				6.70
Penicillin or Streptomycin				
Intravenous Solutions				
Oxygen				
Circumcision				2.00
		TOTAL CHARGES		92.70
		TOTAL CREDITS		
		BALANCE — AMOUNT DUE		

Should this statement be in error, kindly so advise, that we may rectify it.

Form 805-A — P.R.Co.-1106-750-6M

bringing home baby

This is a bill my wife and I received from the hospital when our son was born in 1950. I was told that I could not take the baby home until I paid in full! We were short on money at the time, so my father cut the check to the hospital. It must have cleared, as we've been enjoying our son ever since.

— *Ken Nelson, Kenosha, Wisconsin*

make time for TV

TV brought the world into our living rooms. Folks who had never set foot outside their towns were transported to exotic lands they could never hope to visit.

In less serious moments, TV introduced us to comedians like Jackie Gleason, Lucille Ball and Jack Benny, as well as variety shows like *Toast of the Town* with Ed Sullivan.

Here are more memories from *Reminisce* readers who remember television's early days....

One of the Family

Sharply dressed and ready for church, here are my father, Jim Heyboer; brother, Jimmy; and I (below). In the background, you can see the newest member of the family—our first television set! It was really a TV, radio and record player all in one. My mother used to say that all they did was pay to have the television repaired, but we were still proud to call it ours.

One more interesting note...the dress I'm wearing cost $1 and was made of plastic!
— *Joan Meyer, Grand Rapids, Michigan*

TV—and Dignity— 'Repossessed'

Television sets were expensive in the early '50s, so most people could not afford them. But my family was lucky to have many models of General Electric TV sets courtesy of (and unbeknownst to) the GE Company.

My dad, Bob Colvig, worked in the carpentry department for GE in Liverpool, New York. His job was to build the sets for the GE "House of Magic" display at the New York State Fair in Syracuse. He also designed and built cabinetry for the clock radios and TVs.

Dad was friends with Charlie Ranger, the driver for one of the GE executives. Charlie would sometimes hang out and drink coffee at the carpenter shop between chauffeuring duties. At times, Dad found he had more TV sets than he could work on, so he would ask Charlie to deliver one to our house until he needed it again. Our family would sporadically be able to watch our favorite TV shows, including *Sergeant Preston of the Yukon*, *Sky King* and *Howdy Doody*—that is, until Dad had Charlie come pick up the set and take it back for a new cabinet.

On a day when there was no school in session and everyone on our street was home, Charlie— dressed in his chauffeur's

Trivia Prize Wasn't Trivial

One summer afternoon back in the mid-1950s, my brother, Bob, and I were playing with friends in our front yard when a car drove up. A man got out and asked if he could speak to the lady of the house. We took the man into our house and he explained to our mom that he was representing Folgers Coffee. If she had an unopened can of Folgers that she would open in front of him and then answer a trivia question correctly, she would win a new washing machine!

Mother went down into the basement to a shelf where canned goods were stored and found a dusty can of Folgers. She brought it up and opened it for the man as directed.

Then he asked this trivia »

uniform—came to pick up a set. As he struggled down the front steps with the heavy TV set, he saw many neighbors peeking out doors and standing in driveways watching what was going on at our house.

Never one to miss a perfect opportunity to tease, he yelled out to my mom for all to hear: "Sorry you couldn't pay for your TV set, Mrs. Colvig!" It took Mom a long while to live that one down.

— *Marthe Hildreth, Sarasota, Florida*

Wrestling with Reality

My oldest brother, who was living at home at the time, bought a TV. Only two bars in our small town owned sets. There wasn't much on to watch, but my parents' friends came and filled every inch of the living room. They watched wrestling on the tiny set and loved it.

However, my next brother then went off to college and joined the wrestling team. My mother was horrified! She wouldn't listen when my brother tried to explain that collegiate wrestling was different from the "show" professional type on TV. She would not attend any of my brother's meets during his college years…thus proving the awesome power of the tube.

— *Jean Moon, Upper Sandusky, Ohio*

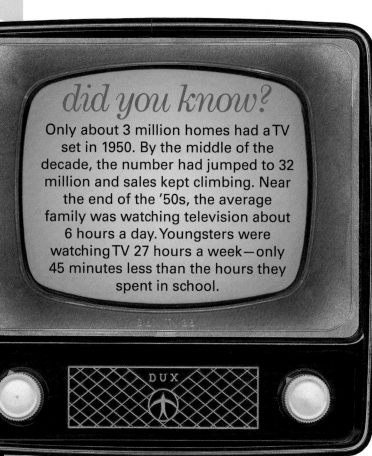

did you know?

Only about 3 million homes had a TV set in 1950. By the middle of the decade, the number had jumped to 32 million and sales kept climbing. Near the end of the '50s, the average family was watching television about 6 hours a day. Youngsters were watching TV 27 hours a week—only 45 minutes less than the hours they spent in school.

Back to the Books

In September 1954, my husband and I settled in Denver, Colorado after working overseas for 3 years. We bought a black-and-white TV, our first set. I had just started a diary, and the first 14 entries are the same: "Had dinner at 6, watched TV." The 15th entry read: "Had dinner at 6. TV broken. Read a book."

— *Pearl Wahler*
Loveland, Colorado

Eyewitness News

We were living in Eustis, Nebraska in 1955 when we purchased our first TV. The large box with a 19-inch screen dominated our living room.

The first night we had the set, I was scurrying naked from my bath to the bedroom.

Just as I stepped into the living room, the 10 o'clock news came on, and there was a close-up of the announcer looking straight at me. Horribly embarrassed, I stopped dead still, then ran back to the bathroom for a towel!

— *Helen Crawford, Shirley, Arkansas*

question: "Who plays Joe Friday on *Dragnet*?" Before she could say a thing, my brother piped up with, "Jack Webb!" Since that was the correct answer, Mom won the washer.

The only problem was that we had recently purchased a new washing machine and Mother didn't want to replace it. The store where the washer was to come from agreed to let us have a new television instead. It was a very nice 21-inch Motorola. At the time, we were the last family in our neighborhood to get a TV, so it was an exciting addition to our home.

Before the man left, my mother asked him why he happened to stop at our house. He said it was because of all the kids in our yard. He thought we were a large family and could probably use a new washing machine. Our family enjoyed the television set we got instead for many years.

— *Gayle Krause, Tacoma, Washington*

Remember Saying?

ginchiest

Best, Coolest

growing up with Grandma

In the '50s, relatives were often around to help Mom and Dad out with the children. Here's such a scene as Mindy Sue Button, age 5, and David McKinley Button, 1 month, pose with their grandmother on a warm summer day in 1957.

— *David Button, Roswell, New Mexico*

the convenient kitchen

ADVERTISERS OFFERED '50s HOUSEWIVES LABOR-SAVING APPLIANCES AND QUICK-AND-EASY FOODS.

Can you identify this person? She's wearing a dress, ruffled apron, heels and a cheerful smile. She's tidied the house, fixed a home-cooked meal, freshened up, seated her children at the table and now awaits the return of her hardworking husband from a long day at the office.

Figure it out? She's the ideal housewife of the 1950s—as imagined by the media at the time. She's also known by *Time* magazine as "the keeper of the suburban dream." The '50s homemaker had a lot on her plate, and appliance and food manufacturers were happy to lighten her load.

Appliances Aplenty

From toasters to stand mixers to ranges, electric appliances promised convenience, efficiency and styling. Magazine ads touted the benefits of kitchen items that, as one cookware manufacturer assured, would establish a woman's "reputation as a fine cook and clever hostess."

International Harvester refrigerators were "femineered," offering "scores of chore-saving, women-approved features." General Electric automatic dishwashers promised to save "over 200 hours of work a year." The Presto electric pressure cooker assured busy cooks they could fix Sunday menus any day of the week, because the time-saving appliance did "an hour's cooking in 20 minutes!"

"Automatically" was the word of the day. Servel offered "the world's only refrigerator that makes a continuous supply of ice cubes without trays automatically!" Sunbeam's waffle maker made "four good-sized waffles at one time...automatically!" And West Bend's Flavo-Matic electric percolator was "nearly magic the way it automatically brews the best tasting coffee ever!"

The New "Fast Food"

The '50s cook was encouraged to trim time from meal preparation with convenience foods, "ready mixes," canned goods and frozen foods. Advertisers emphasized the ease of preparation—not always flavor. Among the new "in a jiffy" food items introduced during this decade were Minute Rice, Mrs. Paul's fish sticks, Lipton dehydrated onion soup mix, Cheez Whiz, Tang breakfast drink, Duncan Hines cake mixes, Green Giant canned beans

Can I Lick the Beaters?

As soon as my wife took out the Mixmaster, there were three little helpers propped up on chairs, fascinated by the whole procedure. This 1953 photo shows our kids getting into the action.

— *Calvin Glazier, Leverett, Massachusetts*

Oven Fresh

This picture of my son, Gary, and I advertised a local bakery's brown-and-serve rolls and appeared in our newspaper in June 1950. Gary still has this smile on his face whenever he returns home to enjoy his mother's home cooking.

— *Gene Marsh, Knoxville, Tennessee*

and Rice-A-Roni.

Print and broadcast advertising boosted items launched years earlier, such as Campbell's condensed soups. Cream soups were a mainstay of such dinner delights as Tuna Noodle Casserole, meatloaf "frosted" with mashed potatoes, and Green Bean Casserole, which was created in 1955 and remains popular today.

Other quick-and-easy recipes in ads included Fiesta Peach Spam Bake, using Spam canned meat and canned peaches; Pie Plate Salad, blending Veg-All canned mixed vegetables with lemon gelatin; and Tuna-Rice Au Gratin, with Minute Rice and Carnation evaporated milk.

Even better than canned foods, frozen foods—from juices to vegetables to fish— were promoted as the ultimate in convenience. In 1954, as television moved into more American homes, Swanson TV dinners were introduced. Ads proclaimed: "No work before…no dishes after! But what a meal!" Indeed, the partitioned aluminum trays with meat, potato and vegetables were ready to pop in the oven…and enjoy during your favorite TV show.

Homemade With Love

Though ads lauded shortcut suppers, many home cooks continued to prepare simple meals from scratch. Betty Crocker's Picture Cookbook from 1950 includes pot roast, savory stew, fried chicken and plenty of other traditional fare. And any child of the '50s probably remembers the heavenly

aroma of homemade cakes and cookies in the kitchen.

Sunday dinner, usually served around midday or after church, was sacred in many homes. Usually a meat-and-potatoes affair, it offered families an opportunity to sit around the table and connect. Children were expected to be neatly dressed and to help clean up. And rarely, if ever, were »

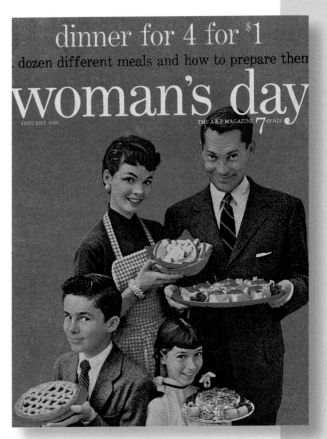

Woman's Day, circa 1956

Food at the Ready

In the '50s, plastics—particularly Tupperware—helped the home cook keep her refrigerator and cabinets organized. Tupperware home parties gave homemakers a chance to see the "magic Tupper Seal" demonstrated, to socialize and to make a little money in the process.

preferences indulged. Clean plates were expected, while moms across the country perfected their guilt-inducing "There are starving children in China" speech.

American takes on foreign cuisine emerged. Soldiers returning from faraway lands developed new tastes for ethnic foods,

so suburban housewives obliged with watered-down versions of chop suey, French pilaf, Spanish rice, curried lamb and Polynesian fare, spurring an interest in canned pineapple (pineapple upside-down cake, anyone?) and exciting presentation techniques like flambé.

While some will recall the decade for onion-soup dip and weird molded salads, others will remember the care home cooks put into family dinners. But there's one thing everyone can agree on…food was surely a fun part of the '50s.

kidding around

I loved olives as a kid—eaten properly off the fingers, of course. Here's a picture of my mom, Joan, and me at an after-church supper with the family in the spring of '59.

—Peggy Oels
Phoenix, Arizona

circa 1950

Household, circa 1952

Convenient canned goods and "time-saving" appliances were kitchen staples in the '50s, as these advertisements show.

Rockford Register - Republic, circa 1954

pass your plate

A good crowd was gathered at the Staffords' home in 1957 for this family feast. Our cousins and aunt came to our house because there were too many Staffords to take to the others' houses. Among those pictured are (counterclockwise, starting with girl in blue dress) my cousin Nancy Stonehouse; my brother Ronnie; my sister Judy; my mother's godfather, Mr. Arnold; my great-great-aunt Eula Colgate; my brother Norman; my brother Artie; me and my father, Norman.

— *Norma Jean Hissong, Olympia, Washington*

CHAPTER FOUR

Pop!

Actress Mary Martin's career was flying high after starring in *Peter Pan* on Broadway in 1954. And Max Brunswick of New Haven, Connecticut will never forget how he gave her a lift—even if it was only in an elevator.

"In high school, I was an usher at the Loew's Poli Theatre, the biggest movie house in Connecticut," Brunswick recalls. "I got paid 75 cents an hour and could see all the movies I wanted for free."

One day in 1957, Brunswick was told that Harry Shaw, the big kahuna of all the Loew's theaters, wanted a uniformed usher to run the elevator for a visiting star: one Mary Martin.

If Brunswick was speechless at sharing an elevator with the world-famous actress, it didn't matter; he had orders to remain silent—no requests for autographs allowed.

"So I just stood there at attention," Brunswick says.

For his service, he didn't even get a tip. "Elevator operators didn't get tips then," he explains.

Brunswick wasn't the only kid who encountered celebrities in the 1950s. For more star-studded memories of pop culture in this decade, read on....

Behind the Scenes with Lucy

A YOUNG BOY ENJOYS A RARE BIRD'S-EYE VIEW OF THE *I LOVE LUCY* SET AND WITNESSES TELEVISION HISTORY IN THE MAKING.

By Gregg Oppenheimer, Santa Monica, California

I can remember, as a kid, sitting at the very top of the wooden bleachers in the darkened soundstage at Desilu Studios, watching as they filmed *I Love Lucy*.

My father, Jess Oppenheimer, was the show's producer and head writer. He told me I had the best seat in the house—not in the first row but the last, high enough to see over the three huge Mitchell cameras that constantly maneuvered for position in and around the Ricardos' apartment.

My first visit to the set was when I was 4 years old, too young to realize what a huge star Lucille Ball was.

When Dad introduced me, I just stared at her incredibly red hair. Kneeling down, she flashed me that famous smile and asked, "Where did you get those big brown eyes?" Still staring, I said, "They came with the face." Lucy and my father rocked with laughter.

At the time, of course, I had no idea that I was behind the scenes at the creation of the most influential series in television history. But then again, neither did anyone else.

"We were an eager and innocent crew," Dad later recalled, "embarking on a trip in a medium about which we knew nothing. None of us had any inkling of the high-flying success that lay ahead.

"We all were just knocking ourselves out to put the show on the air each week. What's more, we loved the work—none of us could wait to get to the set or the typewriter."

The biggest reason for this inspiration was the radiant talent of Lucille Ball. As Dad put it, "The audience never had the »

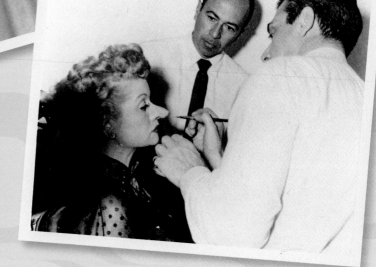

HIGH UP. Here's how the set of *I Love Lucy* looked from the studio bleachers (top). Famous funny scenes from the show include grape-stomping Lucy and Vitameatavegamin pitchwoman Lucy. At right, she's getting her putty nose for a scene with William Holden as author's dad looks on.

Pop!

feeling they were watching her act. She simply was Lucy Ricardo."

And, as Lucy Ricardo, she did every stunt written for her. Occasionally, though, it took some persuasion. In the first of the "Hollywood" episodes, William Holden visits the Ricardos' hotel room after an unfortunate encounter at the Brown Derby, and Lucy disguises herself with kerchief, glasses and a long putty nose.

The script called for the end of Lucy's nose to go up in flames when Holden lights her cigarette. It took Dad all week to convince Lucy that her real nose wouldn't also catch fire.

The makeup man used a special putty nose with a wick in it to ensure her safety. Still, Lucy was nervous all through rehearsal and during the final shooting.

When her putty nose caught fire, she was supposed to remove it and dunk it into her coffee. Instead, Lucy ad-libbed and picked up the cup with both hands, dunking the end of her putty nose while it was still attached. It was an inspired moment—entirely hers.

I Love Lucy looks so good today that it's hard to believe it was produced at a time

Cover Girl

Lucille Ball was on the very first cover of *TV Guide* and has been on the cover more times than any other person.

Source: *Lucilleball.com*

when relatively few people had TV sets. In fact, when Jerry Hausner won the role of Ricky's agent, the actor worried that his own father wouldn't even get to see his performance.

Until then, the only television Jerry's father had ever seen was the one in the front window of a furniture store on Hollywood Boulevard. Every Friday night, he'd stand outside and watch the wrestling matches. Of course, he couldn't hear anything through the thick plate glass, but that wasn't important with wrestling.

So when Jerry offered to buy his father a TV set, he was shocked that his dad turned him down.

"Not yet," Jerry's father advised. "Wait till they get sound. They'll figure it out one of these days, just like they did with the movies."

When writing the show, Dad couldn't resist the temptation to mention me and my sister Joanne by name sometimes. I still get a kick out of hearing Lucy tell Ricky she had decided on the perfect name for the baby— "Gregory if it's a boy and Joanne if it's a girl."

It almost makes me feel as though I'm back at Desilu.

Remember Saying?

big tickle

Really funny

Did You Know?

✶ Within 5 months of its October 1951 debut, *I Love Lucy* was the top-rated show on TV. Except for the 1955-'56 season (when it was beaten by *The $64,000 Question*), it held onto that spot for the rest of its run.

✶ It was the first TV program to be filmed by three moving cameras before a live audience—a system still used today.

✶ The show wasn't just black and white on television. Karl Freund, director of photography, had the set for the Ricardos' New York apartment painted in shades of gray because he'd just devised a "flat lighting" system for three moving cameras and didn't want to have to worry about how colors would translate onto black-and-white TV sets.

✶ Lucy and Desi were originally "Lucy and Larry Lopez." Those names were changed at the last minute so viewers wouldn't confuse Desi with then-popular bandleader Vincent Lopez.

✶ Although it was the most influential and imitated sitcom in TV history, the show never won a single Emmy Award for writing. Nominated twice, Lucy's writers lost out to *The George Gobel Show* in 1954 and *You'll Never Get Rich* in 1955.

✶ When the cameras weren't rolling, Vivian Vance ("Ethel Mertz") and William Frawley ("Fred Mertz") didn't care for one another.

✶ Saturday-afternoon reruns of *I Love Lucy* placed among the top 10 television shows in 1955, tying with first-run, prime-time episodes of *The Honeymooners*.

De Agostini/SuperStock

journal entry

my favorite '50s
TV stars

television

In the 1950s, home entertainment was radically transformed as television turned the dial down on radio. The new medium caught on so fast it was reported that children were spending more hours in front of the tube than in school!

The allure is understandable. *I Love Lucy*, *The $64,000 Question* and *The Mickey Mouse Club* were irresistibly entertaining.

Variety shows ruled. Americans couldn't get enough of live, vaudeville-inspired programs hosted by the likes of Milton Berle, Ed Sullivan, Jack Benny and George Gobel. ABC, NBC, CBS and the old DuMont network were happy to oblige.

By the end of the decade girls swooned over TV celebs like Ricky Nelson, young boys idolized Davy Crockett, cowboy wannabes loyally followed *Gunsmoke* and everybody danced along with Dick Clark and his *American Bandstand*.

Jack Benny

Photos 12/Alamy

Dick Clark

Visions of America, LLC/Alamy

an American icon

My father, Joseph Spinale, met Ed Sullivan in 1952 while working as a page at the Copley Plaza Hotel in Boston. Although he met many famous people, Dad was especially excited to meet the host of one of our family's favorite shows, *Toast of the Town*.

—*Joseph Spinale Jr., Radcliffe, Kentucky*

A visit from Bob Hope and Marilyn Maxwell in Pyongyang, North Korea was the best holiday present this 19-year-old Army combat correspondent (far right) ever could have imagined. Also pictured is Major Carmen Rossi.

a soldier's memory

By Charles Barbour, Durham, North Carolina

I will never forget when Bob Hope visited the 1st Cavalry Division during the holidays in the North Korean capital of Pyongyang and how much it meant to me and the troops.

Bob Hope, Marilyn Maxwell, Jerry Colonna, the Taylor Maids and others arrived in Pyongyang not long after we had taken and secured the city. Their visit was a nice holiday present for those of us so far north of the 38th parallel.

But it was even more memorable for me, a 19-year-old Army combat correspondent who was named to accompany the performers during their stay. Today, when I think of Korea in 1950 and '51, my thoughts inevitably turn to the entertainers' visit. It's a perfect antidote for my wartime visions of destruction.

Sadly, the troupe left after two days and nights for a command performance on a ship involved in the amphibious landing at Inchon.

I'll never forget when Marilyn Maxwell gave me both her fur-lined parka and a goodbye kiss smack on the lips. I have never been able to decide which kept me warmer on those cold winter nights after she left—the parka or kiss.

That visit is something I'll cherish for a lifetime.

good nights with "Uncle Miltie"

By Maxine Averbuck, Sebastopol, California

With our first television set in 1950 came some lifestyle changes at our Long Beach, California home. One rule held fast, though—an early bedtime for my brother, Treuman, and me on weeknights.

Occasionally I'd plead the case for extending my bedtime, but Dad was adamant. Worse yet, even though I couldn't see those evening programs, I could hear the tantalizing audio from my bedroom.

The show I wanted most to see was Milton Berle's *Texaco Star Theater*. When I heard the opening theme song, "Oh, we're the men from Texaco, we work from Maine to Mexico…," I was in sheer agony.

All that laughter—both from the audience and my parents—made me yearn to see what was so funny.

One Tuesday night, I crept out of bed and tiptoed down the hall. After crouching in the doorway to the den, I crawled to a spot where a lamp table separated Dad's recliner and Mom's chair. I lay on my stomach so I could see the TV screen between the legs of the table.

When I thought the show was nearly over, I started crawling back to my room. Unfortunately, I hit my head on the table, shaking the lamp.

"What was that?" Mom asked, swinging around in her chair.

Dad tilted his recliner all the way back and, turning his head, looked right into my face. "Seems we have a visitor."

"Maxine!" Mom got out of her chair and came over to me. "What in the world?"

Tears welled up in my eyes. After

TRIPLE THREAT. Uncle Miltie could act the clown or dance with the gals, but he was known in the business as an incredibly hard worker.

making sure I wasn't hurt, Mom sat down and hoisted me onto her lap. "Sit here with me for a few minutes and you'll feel better," she said.

Sitting on Mom's lap, I pretended not to watch the TV…but when Uncle Miltie did a sketch about Charlie Chan's No. 1 son, I started giggling. Soon all three of us were howling with laughter.

When the show was over, Mom tucked me into bed. "Don't say anything about this to your brother," she warned.

"Can I see Uncle Miltie again?" I asked.

"Dad and I will talk about it," she replied.

The next Tuesday as Mom tucked me in, she said, "Promise me that you won't sneak out again, Maxine."

I pouted. "Oh, Mama…why can't I watch Uncle Miltie? I'll be lying awake listening anyway."

Mom smiled. "When the show starts, I'll come and see if you're awake. If you are, then you can come and watch."

I lay there repeating poems and telling myself stories, trying to stay awake. Suddenly I heard the show's opening song. Had I fallen asleep?

I quickly sat up in bed and saw Mom in the doorway, beckoning with her finger. "Shhh," she whispered. "We don't want to wake your brother."

It was wonderful. I couldn't believe all the facial expressions Uncle Miltie had.

Our routine continued each week after that. If I was still awake when the show started, I got to watch with Mom and Dad.

This went on until I was 13 and allowed to stay up later than my brother. Then, one Tuesday night, we were watching Uncle Miltie and heard a thump.

It was my brother, attempting to sneak back to bed—he'd just bumped his head on the table by Dad's recliner.

serious serendipity

By Elaine Nemer, Kenner, Louisiana

We loved visiting Las Vegas while my husband, Joe, was stationed at Travis Air Force Base in California. During a visit in 1958, we noticed that superstar Danny Thomas was appearing at the Sands Hotel.

When we arrived, however, we learned the show was sold out. Disappointed and dejected, we went back outside. As we debated what to do next, I looked up and saw Danny Thomas walking our way. I couldn't believe it!

When he got near us, we stopped him and struck up a conversation by mentioning that we have relatives in Toledo, Ohio, where Thomas grew up. By coincidence, he actually knew them! Then I quickly chimed in that we wanted to see his show but it was sold out. We couldn't believe it when he said he'd reserve us tickets for the late show.

That night, we picked up our tickets and were seated at a table by the stage. It was a great dinner and a great show that we'll always remember.

Strangely enough, we again ran into Thomas some 30 years later, outside a Los Angeles restaurant called Chasen's, where many stars ate. We reminded him of that day 30 years earlier when he got a young first lieutenant and his wife tickets for a show. We'll never forget those two chance meetings with this gracious celebrity.

Remember Saying?

radioactive

Popular

movies & stage

All the world was a stage in the fabulous '50s, and silver screen stars like Elizabeth Taylor, Marilyn Monroe, Cary Grant and Marlon Brando knew how to light it up.

Film favorites from the decade include *The Creature from the Black Lagoon*, *White Christmas*, *Guys and Dolls*, *Gentlemen Prefer Blondes*, *An American in Paris*, *A Streetcar Named Desire*, *Oklahoma!*, *Love Me Tender*, *Around the World in 80 Days*, *The King and I*, *The 10 Commandments*, *Invasion of the Body Snatchers* and *The Bridge on the River Kwai*. Younger moviegoers discovered the power of Disney as *Cinderella*, *Alice in Wonderland*, *Peter Pan* and *Sleeping Beauty* captured their imaginations.

Jump to the East Coast, and fabulous productions like *South Pacific* and *My Fair Lady* dazzled theater audiences on the Great White Way.

Marilyn Monroe

Mary Evans Picture Library/Alamy

Cary Grant

Pictorial Press Ltd/Alamy

Thanks, Mr. President!

By Rosemary Trettin, Appleton, Wisconsin

During vacation from high school teaching in the summer of 1954, I traveled to Glacier National Park in Montana. While there, I stopped at the park lodge to eat.

As I mingled with other travelers, there was an announcement on the public-address system that Ronald Reagan was in the area, filming a western with Barbara Stanwyck, and he was due at the lodge for a lunch break. (I later learned the movie was *Cattle Queen of Montana*.) When Mr. Reagan arrived, I jumped at the chance to ask him if he'd mind posing for a picture. He graciously consented and stood by his car. That's his son in the front seat.

my date
with Marilyn

By Robert Suhosky, Tarzana, California

Marilyn Monroe had a reputation for tardiness, and I learned about it firsthand when we met in September of 1953. Our appointment at the 20th Century Fox studios was for 1 p.m.; Marilyn breezed in at 2:30.

I was a staff sergeant in the Marine Corps and a correspondent for *Leatherneck* magazine, which enabled me to arrange an interview with the woman every serviceman wanted to meet.

It hadn't been easy. "Monroe Mania" was lifting off like a rocket, and there was a waiting list of journalists from around the world.

The day of our interview I was told we had jumped the line, beating out *USS Pittsburgh* and *American Weekly* magazines.

The "we" included me and *Leatherneck* photographer Master Sgt. J.W. Richardson. With as much of a shock of wavy red hair as the Marine Corps would allow, J.W. answered to "Red."

After the formal photo session was over, Marilyn settled into a comfortable chaise. I took a chair opposite, while Red moved around, popping pictures and changing film.

For 3 hours, I asked questions and Marilyn answered sweetly, laughingly and sometimes poignantly.

Yes, she got a lot of mail from Marines. Yes, they wanted photos—autographed. Yes, she received marriage proposals.

I noticed she didn't smoke, even though she had in her recent film, *Niagara*, with Joseph Cotten and Jean Peters. "I had to learn to smoke for the role," Marilyn explained. "But I don't like smoking."

When I asked for her thoughts about going to Korea to entertain the troops, she became serious and said it was something she definitely wanted to do.

I enjoyed myself immensely, but after 3 hours I was out of questions. I thanked Marilyn for her time and got ready to leave.

But Red, who had not said a word, jumped into the act and said, "Ski, sit next to Marilyn and let me take a picture of you."

This photo is the result!

When we finally did say goodbye to Marilyn the day of the interview, there was one last question: "If you're not busy, would you let us invite you to dinner tonight?"

Marilyn's face lit up. "Gee, fellas, I'd love to. But Joe's coming to town tonight. Maybe next time?"

Joe, of course, was "Joltin'" Joe DiMaggio, the "Yankee Clipper," who went to the Far East with Marilyn—on their honeymoon.

There never was a next time.

A Pleasant Meal with Frankenstein

By Corinne DeGeorge, Redding, California

Photos 12/Alamy

In the early 1950s, I worked as a cashier in the cocktail lounge of the Hotel Lawrence in Erie, Pennsylvania. One night, as I was closing up the lounge, I couldn't believe it when actor Boris Karloff, who was appearing in a local stage production of *Arsenic and Old Lace*, came in and asked me to recommend a good place to eat.

I pointed him to a restaurant across the street that was open all night. Then he asked me to join him because he hated to eat alone. I loved watching him in movies, so of course, I agreed.

He was a very kind gentleman; we talked until almost 5 a.m. Then he walked me to my car, gave me a gallant kiss on the hand and departed.

celebrity doorman

By Doris Belovich, Cleveland, Ohio

In the mid-1950s, I got a job at the Cleveland Clinic in Cleveland, working in the pathology laboratory.

One day, we learned that the father of famous actor Jimmy Stewart was coming to our hospital from Indiana, Pennsylvania for possible surgery. We all wondered if the star himself would come to visit his father, and what we would say and do if our paths crossed.

The next day, on the way to lunch, we talked about the possibility of meeting Stewart. In fact, we were so engrossed that we didn't realize until afterward that he had held a door open for us. When we figured out what had happened, we almost died on the spot!

John Springer Collection/CORBIS

92

In the '50s, Whitman's used famous faces like Bob Hope and Elizabeth Taylor to advertise their confections.

music

Established artists like Nat "King" Cole, Perry Como and Louis Armstrong held their own in the '50s, but when Les Paul developed and marketed a solid-bodied Gibson electric guitar around 1952, the music industry was forever changed.

In the middle of the decade, teenagers everywhere spun artists like Fats Domino, Chuck Berry and "the King."

Elvis Presley released a dozen No. 1 hits from 1950 to 1959, including *Love Me Tender*, *Heartbreak Hotel* and *Hound Dog*. In 1958, hits like *Don't* and *King Creole* came out right before Elvis became an Army private.

Other rock artists on the scene were the Everly Brothers with hits like *Bye Bye Love* and *Wake Up Little Susie*, Jerry Lee Lewis with *Whole Lot of Shakin' Going On* and Little Richard with *Lucille*.

And who could ever forget these all-the-rage ditties: *My Foolish Heart*; *Luck Be a Lady*; *A Bushel and a Peck*; *Cry Me a River*; *Love and Marriage*; *Dance With Me*; *I Walk the Line*; *The Purple People Eater*; *Tequila*; *Papa Loves Mambo*; and *Shake, Rattle, and Roll*.

Everly Brothers

Pictorial Press Ltd./Alamy

Chuck Berry

Pictorial Press Ltd./Alamy

Book Him!

This 1958 photo shows the "Keystone Kops" from the American Legion Milwaukee Police Post 415. The paddy wagon was used as a fundraiser for the March of Dimes. Here, Gus Bergemann escorts well-known singer and actor Eddie Fisher to the back of the vehicle with the help of Frank Groeschel and Art Rinderle.

Post 415 bought the 1935 GMC paddy wagon in the 1940s from the Milwaukee Police Department. It made an appearance in the 1991 TV movie *Dillinger* and to this day is rolled out for parades and car shows.

—*Donald Brockman, Milwaukee, Wisconsin*

a happy accident

By Gene Campbell, Arlington, Texas

I grew up in Happy, Texas. While attending West Texas State University in the mid-1950s, I met another guy from Happy: rockabilly star Buddy Knox.

I sang in the school's Hi Fi Quartet, and Buddy asked me to join the Serenaders—a group he organized to serenade coeds. Sometimes Buddy would invite me and other musical friends to join him at nearby Buffalo Lake, where we'd build a fire and sing songs. His sister, Verdi, and some of the school's cheerleaders would be there, too.

Back then, Buddy sang his songs— including his big hit, *Party Doll*—as ballads, not rock 'n' roll songs. But he was already fascinated with a budding star by the name of Elvis Presley, whom he later befriended in the U.S. Army. As for me, I dismissed rock 'n' roll as a passing craze. Guess I was off on that one!

It was around this time that Buddy recorded *Party Doll*, accompanied by Verdi and some other WTSU coeds. He also appeared on *The Ed Sullivan Show* and *The Steve Allen Show*. To hang with this future star was quite a thrill for a small-town kid like me.

Michael Ochs Archives/Stringer/Getty

journal entry

my '50s music memories

dressed-down celebrity

By Greta Bryan
Yakima, Washington

My husband, Hal, and his friend, Scott Mason, worked in Fort Worth, Texas, during the summer of 1956. They hung awnings for Scott's uncle Miller Burch, who sold and rented high-end patio furniture.

That summer, Liberace was in town to perform in the stage play *The Great Waltz*. One of the scenes required patio furniture, which led the show's producer to Uncle Miller's business.

Uncle Miller agreed to provide the furniture for free, under one condition: that Scott, Hal and their girlfriends—Elaine Lucas and I—could meet Liberace after an evening performance. The producer agreed.

On the assigned night, the four of us excitedly headed backstage after the show, only to discover that our meeting was supposed to occur the next night. Disappointed, we said we wouldn't be able to make it. So, as you can see in this photo, the star graciously agreed to see us anyway—and take a photo with us (Hal and I are to Liberace's left), even though he was in his dressing gown!

Remember Saying?

sides

Vinyl records

Perfect Pitch

By Albert Martinez, Commerce, California

I'll never forget the summer of 1956, when Lawrence Welk played my accordion, accompanied by the junior accordion band that I directed in Encino, California.

It happened at the opening game of our Little League season. I had led the band out in center field to play the national anthem. When we finished, we traipsed back to the area around home plate and—lo and behold—there was Welk, shaking hands with people attending the opening ceremonies.

I was introduced to the legendary bandleader, who was duly impressed with our young accordionists. In fact, he was as cordial as could be. He beamed, much like a politician running for office—except that he was truly sincere!

Soon people asked Welk to play the accordion with our junior band. He begged off, saying he didn't have his accordion with him. I told him he could use mine—and he did! It came off very well; Welk was a deft player. And you can imagine how proud the parents of our band members felt!

this kiss was bliss

By Jean Porcasi, Hicksville, New York

My favorite summer was in 1952, when my parents took me on a 2-week vacation to Marlboro, New York after I graduated from eighth grade.

Early one afternoon, while we were at a local Italian restaurant, singing star Julius La Rosa drove up in a beautiful red convertible, accompanied by singer Lu Ann Simms. I was thrilled to see this singer, who at that time was very popular. I couldn't believe it when he gave me his autograph—and a kiss on the cheek. I was so excited to be kissed by an actual celebrity! I'll always remember that summer.

dinner with Elvis

By Jules Archer, Scotts Valley, California

In 1956, I got the chance to spend a few days with Elvis Presley while he was making his first movie. I was a reporter then, and my assignment was to interview this rock 'n' roll sensation.

Along with most American parents of that day, I was prejudiced against the 21-year-old teen idol. He seemed a "delinquent" type.

I had my doubts about his music, too.

My attitude was shared by most of the actors waiting for Elvis to appear on the 20th Century Fox set of *Love Me Tender*.

Later, as I watched Elvis shoot scenes with his co-star, Debra Paget, I was struck by the fact that he was more handsome in real life. And I was impressed that he played mumblety-peg between takes with members of the crew as if he were just one of them.

"The kid surprised us all," one of the actors told me. "He turned out to be the most warmhearted kid you ever saw."

During a break, I approached Elvis for the interview. Sizing me up with his blue eyes, he suggested having dinner in his hotel suite.

When I showed up, Elvis greeted me warmly. Then he said a little hesitantly: "Mr. Archer, I hope you're not going to make up a lot of things I never said. A lot of other writers have done that to me."

"Elvis," I assured him, "there won't be a word in my story that you haven't told me."

I kept my word on that, and he later showed his appreciation by giving me a copy of his *Elvis* album, inscribing it, "For Jules, one of the nicest guys I ever met."

As we conversed, I found him to be an everyday boy from the Mississippi Delta.

I learned that he didn't drink or smoke, was bored by nightclubs, and relaxed by throwing baseballs at wooden milk bottles and winning teddy bears. Deeply religious, he frequently grew lonesome away from his parents.

Elvis was truly one of the nicest youths I'd ever met—certainly one of the most polite and most respectful.

'The King' and I

In 1957, my husband, Norm, was a disc jockey at CKDA, a radio station in Victoria, British Columbia. Before he was inducted into the Army, Elvis Presley scheduled one last show in Vancouver, which happened to be his only one outside the U.S.
The big night arrived and Norm arranged for three busloads of fans to attend the show. I was fortunate enough to get backstage as Norm interviewed "the King." We are both retired now and have wonderful memories of that night.

—*Elsie Pringle, Winnetka, California*

CHAPTER FIVE

Fashion flashback

When gals in the '50s found themselves perplexed about all things fashionable, they could ask themselves a simple question: What would Audrey or Doris wear?

"Audrey Hepburn and Doris Day were our models," recalls Blanche Comiskey of Greendale, Wisconsin. "Hepburn was glamorous and Day was pretty and perky."

In the Eisenhower era, formal usually trumped casual. Whether it was a Saturday-night party or church on Sunday morning, 1950s fashionistas wore a fancy hat, a calf-length dress and high-heeled shoes with rounded "peep" toes. Even a fun jaunt on a train from Comiskey's hometown of Duluth, Minnesota to the Twin Cities required at least a dressy full skirt and a button-down blouse with a rounded Peter Pan collar, Comiskey says.

For less formal occasions, poodle skirts and saddle shoes were big. And for hanging around with gal pals, penny loafers and jeans with rolled-up cuffs were the cat's meow. Top it all off with a bouffant hairdo, and a girl had it made.

Turn the page to see what other fashions were all the rage....

Everett Collection

Catalog Couture

A VINTAGE SEARS CATALOG SPURS MEMORIES OF THE STYLISH, SOPHISTICATED '50s.

By JoAnn Adams, San Pedro, California

Flipping through a 1950s Sears catalog at an antique shop, I was struck by the black-and-white photo of neckties on page 116. When I was 10 years old, those bold geometric prints on a wide swath of silk pulled my focus from my cornflakes each morning to the starched white cotton of my dad's shirts. Dad always looked dapper and ready for work in his wool suit and vest. And from the catalog, I learned it cost $23.95 to look that stylish in a suit.

That brief look back rekindled my interest in that decade. I've always been curious about the things my mom might have been doing when I was a child, so I purchased the catalog.

I recall Mom in the heavily starched and perfectly pressed cotton housedresses she wore daily. Even doing housework, she looked so ladylike and proper. I imagined she would finish some cleaning chore and take a break to page through the catalog. So I spent an afternoon doing the same, picturing myself in her place, shopping and ordering clothes for our family.

On page 1, the featured dress and jacket with its Scotty cap could be very cute on me—even today! The price was $5.98, and since I really liked the Shetland wool hat with plaid streamers, I would buy that too, at 99 cents extra.

"Moonglow," an evening gown shown on

SEARS STYLE. Author JoAnn Adams (front left) with her sister, Iris, and her parents in front of the family's Los Angeles home. Dad is wearing a suit and tie the author recognized in a vintage 1950s Sears catalog.

page 5, featured a shirred bodice to give me "flattering fullness" (I've always needed that) and a set-in girdle to "make (my) waistline look tiny" (I've always wanted that, too). Artificial flowers to tuck in my hair came with the long gown, available in sunset rose, royal blue and aqua at $2.98.

Several pages later, I find girdles...and I am so glad they fell out of fashion. I can still remember Mom struggling in and out of hers. And to think it cost $5.88 to suffer that sort of discomfort.

My sister, Iris, and I were often dressed

FASHION THROUGH THE PAGES. Author JoAnn Adams remembers the decade-defining style of the 1950s as she pages through a vintage clothing catalog, much like this 1952-'53 Fall and Winter edition from Montgomery Ward department store.

alike. When I turn to page 31, I see sweet white dresses with ruffles that look nearly identical to the matching ones my mom bought for us. I remember my mom's friends exclaiming how adorable Iris looked. I decided it was because she was 2 years old, and somehow that was cuter than being 8 years old and in the same dress.

Although my sister and I weren't teenagers at the time, it's fun to see the "smooth and dreamy" dresses that girls in the '50s wore to dazzle their dates for $4.98. The necklines start at the neck (an interesting concept these days), the sleeves cover the upper arm and the hemline is below the knee.

Likewise, maternity wear was a far cry from today's revealing fashions. Dresses, at $2.98, show a very high neckline and pleats from above the bust to below the knee.

PRETTY AS A PICTURE. JoAnn and Iris pose in matching ruffled dresses, also similar to those in the catalog.

Quite a contrast with today's spandex T-shirts, which allow strangers to predict the mom-to-be's exact week of gestation.

Skimming through the catalog, I recognize brand names like Lilly Daché (nets to glamorize ladies' hair), Kerrybrooke (a quality label for Sears) and clothes made with Sanforized fabric, which meant shrinkage was held to 1 percent.

Mickey Mouse, in an earlier incarnation, appears on T-shirts for 98 cents. Apparently, Disneyland pricing has since inflated the cost considerably.

By the end of the afternoon, I'd compiled quite a long list of items to buy. Fortunately, in the '50s, there was an easy payment plan to help finance my purchases.

Remember Saying?

threads

Clothing

DISCOVERED BY PROCTER & GAMBLE

First and only permanent with pin curl <u>ease</u>, rod curl <u>strength</u>

Pin curls for the crown. "Top hair" needs this softer wave...and Lotion plus new Liquifix give longer lasting quality to these pin curls.

Rod curlers for sides, back, top front give added curl-strength to harder-working areas...now doubly reinforced by Lotion and new Liquifix.

Wonderful new soft waves that last and last! A wonderful new method, wonderful new Liquifix. It's here! The first, the only all-over permanent with the ease <u>and</u> the lasting quality you've asked for...yet it's so unbelievably soft and natural. That's because new PIN-IT gives the right kind of waves for the different areas of your hair ...then locks in your permanent with special lotion and new Liquifix neutralizer. Best of all, this new Twice-a-Year PIN-IT keeps your hair just the way you like it, from the first day to months later.

new twice-a-year Pin-it

Apply Lotion and Liquifix with New Target-Point Squeeze Bottle

circa 1958

The Cinderella Project

By Rita Zarlengo, Canfield, Ohio

Our family's Christmas Eve celebration might as well have been a fashion show. Each year, camera bulbs flashed as my aunt Barbra and my cousin Sandy entered my grandmother's house in the small town of Ambridge, Pennsylvania.

Aunt Barbra's blond hair was always impeccably styled in the latest upsweep. Blue-eyed Sandy could have been in a Breck shampoo ad. The ends of her shoulder-length tresses were turned under, and when she moved her head, her hair swayed perfectly.

They were beautiful beyond words, a mother-daughter portrait out of *Vogue*. No one could compare to their perfection—except for the Christmas of 1957, when I was 8.

Preparation for Christmas that year began the weekend after Thanksgiving with the posting of a "to-do" calendar. There were 2 days set aside for me—dress shopping and a Tonette permanent. This was the beginning of the Cinderella Project.

My mother struggled for years with my uncooperative hair. "Your hair is like wire!"

familiar refrain as she tamed my locks with a curling iron from the Dark Ages.

My mother's technique was flawless and my trust in her skill complete, but the results were never as glorious as anticipated. The Tonette perm, however, was sure to be the answer to my woes.

Whoever said, "For beauty, one must suffer," surely had firsthand knowledge of the pain of having the short hairs caught in the rubber-band perm-rod caps, the awful odor of the perm solution and my mother's occasional hair pull if I wriggled in discomfort.

Though I wasn't Cinderella, Mom was more than happy with the almost magical transformation.

That Christmas Eve, my family was the first to arrive for dinner. The best and most predictable comment on the new me came from my grandmother. She really knew how to give a compliment, with a few oohs, aahs and hugs that made me feel so special.

Aunt Barbra and Cousin Sandy were always the last to arrive. My aunt wore a classic long-sleeved navy dress with a fitted skirt that flattered her figure. The seams on her navy hose were so straight you would swear they had been painted on.

The two basked in the family's praise: "You look so pretty!" But apart from my grandmother's glowing words, all I got was a polite, "You look nice."

My Shirley Temple curls never were my favorite, even though I was stuck with them for what seemed like an eternity.

That perm was my last attempt at curls until I was 10. Mom used the perm rods to set my hair for a school picture—and this time captured it forever in black and white.

picture-perfect hat model

By Rena Kerr, Corona Del Mar, California

I'm lucky to have had a wonderful life, and fashion has played a big role in it. In the 1950s, I was a model for the John Robert Powers agency in California and Texas. I also worked for the Harry Conover agency in Los Angeles and Chicago.

I produced fashion shows, did the commentary and modeled as well. We even did swimsuit shows, but the suits were always one-piece—no bikinis!

I gave public lectures about fashion, makeup and the importance of good posture. One of my favorite lines is, "A smile is the most important thing a woman wears."

In those years I appeared on a cover of *Vogue* and an assortment of other magazines.

Hats (and gloves, too) were very popular back then— everyone wore them. There were big hats, small hats, simple hats, fancy jeweled hats and hats in many different shapes and colors. I loved wearing them all.

I still love wearing hats. My house is filled with several hundred. But I don't have the beautiful black hat with pink ruffles and flowers that movie star Cyd Charisse designed for me. I gave it away and miss it to this day!

FEATHER IN HER CAP. Kenneth Hopkins, a California milliner who made hats for *Phantom Lady* and other films of the era, designed this dove-gray hat with a large gray plume, modeled by Rena Kerr. "He was my favorite hat designer, and this is one of my favorites," she says.

HANDMADE HAT. One of the first things Rena Kerr and other models learned to do while training at the John Robert Powers agency was to make a hat in case they needed one. "This is the hat I made—it's black and trimmed with tiny pearls," Kerr notes.

FAMILY FAVORITE. This publicity photo was taken for the California Jewelers' Association's show in downtown Los Angeles. Rena Kerr adds, "This is my son's favorite photo of me. He loves my hair parted in the middle and pulled back into a chignon. It's a great hairstyle for wearing hats."

Big City Shopping

By Mary Lou Sawan, Fredericksburg, Virginia

Today, it seems that shopping is a never-ending chore. But when I was a child in the Baltimore suburb of Catonsville, Maryland, shopping day happened only twice a year—once in spring for Easter and summer clothes, and again in fall for school clothes.

In 1958, at the age of 10, I was becoming less of a tomboy and eagerly anticipated the selection of my Easter outfit.

I felt rather glamorous as we dressed for our adventure in downtown Baltimore. Mom put on her favorite swishy dress, heels, stockings, hat and gloves, and I wore my Sunday best. She fired up the big Oldsmobile and off we went.

When we arrived in the city, we went to Hochschild Kohn, Hutzler's or the Hecht Co. It was like entering a wonderland filled with bright lights, the latest fashions and the smell of all things new.

As the morning wore on, we wandered to the candy counter for a quarter-pound of those round chocolates with white sprinkles on top.

Newly energized, we continued the quest until the perfect Easter outfit came together. It was two pieces, in a navy-blue and white check, with a white collar and a large navy bow at the neck. To accompany it, we picked a white hat with a navy ribbon and black patent leather shoes.

With that done, we were free to concentrate on play clothes to get me

Mary Lou poses in her new Easter outfit—a navy-blue and white check two-piece, with a large navy bow tied at the neck.

through the summer. I don't recall the specifics, but shorts and tops were likely seersucker, because that was my mother's favorite fabric for me.

Around 4 p.m., we returned to the car, our aching arms weighed down by shopping bags. We headed home filled with a satisfaction only females can know.

I loved those special days shopping with my mom. Although she's now gone, I can still remember the sights, sounds, smells and thrill of shopping day.

what the kids were wearing

These readers prove that just because you aren't fully grown doesn't mean you can't be wise in the ways of fashion.

◄ SUN-SUITED

Dressed for some fun in the West Coast sun, these little ladies look adorable in their breezy frocks with frills. "These are our daughters in May 1956," says Arnold McLain of Smithfield, North Carolina. "Debby, on the left, was 3 then and Donna was 1."

◄ HOWDY, PARTNER

Larry Crawford was all duded up in his cowboy outfit for this 1952 photo, while sister Janet stayed with conventional attire. Their brother, Robert Crawford of Apple Valley, Minnesota, shared the slide.

◄ COOL CAT

Cuffed blue jeans, rolled-up sleeves and patterned shirts were all the rage for young men. "This picture was taken at our Bellaire, Ohio home in 1952, when I was 17," says Dick Allietta of Cambridge, Ohio.

◄ POODLE PERFECT

When her daughter, Sherrilyn, wanted a poodle skirt, Opal Turnage of Hawthorne, California, happily obliged by making this fetching creation. Here, Sherrilyn shows off her new frock with her dad and brother, Leamon.

My First Grown-Up Outfit

By Patricia Todd Marshall, Hampton, Virginia

I was raised in the small town of Fox Hill, Virginia. Each year, my parents bought me a new Easter outfit. But in March 1951, I turned 13 and my mom surprised me with something special…my first grown-up outfit!

The navy-blue and white taffeta skirt was paired with a short-sleeved navy taffeta blouse. She also picked out a matching navy purse and hat with netting. But most exciting to me were the blue and white spectator pumps—my first pair of high heels!

I felt so grown-up in the beautiful outfit—much older than 13. I wore it, along with pretty white gloves and some of my mom's jewelry, during Easter week, and often after that to church on Sundays.

The memory of my first grown-up outfit and pair of heels is one I treasure to this day.

GROWN-UP GAL. Author Patricia Todd Marshall, 13, in her navy-blue and white Easter ensemble—including her first pair of high heels—in 1951. She adds, "I wore my hair short and Mom had recently taken me to her beauty parlor for a permanent."

Mom's Crafty Crowns

By Judy Eshleman, Onarga, Illinois

My mother loved crafts. She could always find something to do with whatever material was on hand, wehther it was milkweed pods or driftwood found during one of Dad's fishing trips.

Her downy rabbit-fur hats kept our heads snug in winter. The tam-like caps she made for my sister and me were lined with flannel, with exteriors so nice and soft we felt like bunnies!

Mom found the feathers from the pheasants Dad brought home in their brilliant bronze-reds, browns, purples and greens so beautiful that she just had to use them. She shingled the small feathers over a pillbox form to create a one-of-a-kind crown; adding the colorful cock pheasant's saucy tapering tail as a flourish made it the very definition of panache.

In the 1950s, everyone wore a hat to church and social events. Mom wore her homemade feather hat on those occasions and also fashioned hats for family and friends.

At the time, there was nothing so distinctive as a hat. Do you remember yours?

From the WESTMORES of HOLLYWOOD...
the secret of that glowing "poreless" look!

JANE RUSSELL
RKO star now co-starring in
"GENTLEMEN PREFER BLONDES"
a 20th Century-Fox Picture
Color by Technicolor

World-renowned as the men who make the stars more beautiful, the Westmores are true beauty magicians! Here — with Jane Russell — are Perc Westmore, dean of Hollywood make-up artists; Wally, Make-up Director, Paramount Studios; Frank, famous Hollywood make-up stylist; Bud, Make-up Director, Universal Studios.

DOT! Simply apply a few tiny dots of liquid Tru-Glo to forehead, chin and cheeks.

BLEND! Use fingertips in massaging motion to blend over entire face and under jawline.

PAT! With soft tissue, pat to get "mat" finish. Your complexion becomes luminous and soft!

Follow these 3 MAGIC MAKE-UP STEPS...
for complexion beauty in your own close-ups!

Jane Russell

Miss Russell is using *"Peach Buff"* shade Tru-Glo and *"True Red"* Lipstick.

Yes, *you* can share the make-up secret that gives lovely stars the same glamor on the street that they have in screen close-ups! It's magic Tru-Glo — the fabulous *liquid* make-up created by the Westmores for the stars personally — and for *you!*

Liquid Tru-Glo is easier to apply, longer lasting.

It draws a sheer veil of color over tattle-tale lines, pores, blemishes. Gives your complexion a naturally flawless look all through the day...petal-soft...romantically fresh...radiantly reflecting the "inner" you!

Tru-Glo lures your own true beauty out

of hiding. Perfect for all types of skin. Not greasy, streaky or drying. Comes in shades to suit every skin tone. Get wonderful Tru-Glo today — wherever good cosmetics are sold. See how *easily* the Westmore's 3 magic make-up steps bring your complexion that glowing "poreless" look!

Tru-Glo
LIQUID MAKE-UP

ONLY
59¢
plus tax

Tru-Glo
LIQUID MAKE-UP
Westmore

*Slightly higher in Canada

WESTMORE *Hollywood* **COSMETICS**

Westmores' smear-proof lipstick...
creamy...ravishing!
Match your Tru-Glo complexion with the intoxicatingly vibrant color of Westmores' Hollywood lipstick! Warm and exciting— an invitation to kisses. Stays on longer—won't smudge! Goes on creamy-soft and velvety!

"Creamy Indelible" or *"Regular"*
Only *59¢* plus tax
"Regular" also available at *29¢* plus tax
Also available in Canada

circa 1953

Fashion Flashback

Clothing Fit for a King

By Mary Jane Price, Apple Valley, California

I knew Elvis Presley back when I was 13 and attending Humes High School in Memphis, Tennessee. The first time I met him, I thought he was so handsome!

At the time, I lived across from his house on Alabama Street in North Memphis. He was 4 or 5 years older than me and something of a loner.

Long before he became the king of rock 'n' roll, he dressed the part. He bought his clothes on Beale Street back then, and they were so different from what most other boys wore.

Elvis sported beige trousers, a thin black belt, white suede penny loafers and a black shirt with the collar turned up. His thick dark hair was combed

Everett Collection

into a ducktail with long sideburns. And, as all the girls would say, he had those mysterious, beautiful "bedroom eyes"!

My best friend's sister was about Elvis' age and knew him. Our hangout back then was Thompson's Cafe on Chelsea Avenue. We'd play the jukebox and have Cokes and hamburgers—when we had the money. Hardly anyone had cars, but Elvis would pull alongside us in his old two-seater, and we would just talk and talk!

I love these memories of Elvis, and I love knowing that there was something very special about him even back then.

journal entry

my '50s fashion statements

Remember Saying?

ducktail

Hair combed back into a ridge

Life in the Fabulous '50s

sack it to me!

Thinking "green" isn't new. For decades, folks have been mindful of recycling. Even before the Depression, farm wives took the big sacks that held flour, feed and other consumables and used the cotton fabric to sew household items like curtains and pillowcases, as well as clothing.

During World War II, cotton fabric was in short supply for civilians, so the government promoted the recycling of feed sacks. After the war, national sewing contests were held for women to display their skills and for manufacturers to show off their designs.

Feed-sack clothing remained popular in the 1950s, with poodles and classic cars among the snazzy designs.

▶ SWEET STUFF
In 1952, three bakers' wives showed what could be done with sugar and flour sacks, says Bill Hartmann of Cincinnati, Ohio. From left are Marian Hartmann, Maxine Jennings and Cathy Girmann.

◀ FEEDING THE FAMILY
When Dorothy Caspari of Mountain Home, Arkansas came back from a family visit to Minnesota in the 1950s, she brought along some feed-sack material and used it to make shirts for her two sons.

◀ BEMIS BEAUTIES
Wives and employees of the Bemis Brothers Bag Co. of Wichita, Kansas had a feed-sack dress contest in 1950, says Peggy Garringer of Wichita. Peggy (fifth from left in first row) didn't win, but she certainly had fun making her dress!

what a difference a day makes!

By Vivian Steinmetz, St. Louis, Missouri

These two pictures of my daughters—Dorothy, 7, and Ginnie, 5—were taken a day apart in 1950. My husband, Robert, and I loved to fish. It was the day before Easter and the fish were biting, so we all headed for the river. The girls were dressed in corduroys and home-sewn flannel shirts. They loved to get dirty and muddy, play in the water and sand, catch minnows, handle frogs and show off our latest catch.

Yet as the second photo shows, they still liked to be pretty. Come Easter morning, they wore the outfits I'd made them: purple and green organdy dresses with white panties trimmed with lots of lace. They both had gotten permanents, because that was the style in those days, and they wore matching bows in their hair. That Easter day was as beautiful as the girls.

beauty in a blue dress

This is my bride, Lou, ready to leave on our honeymoon
on September 4, 1954. A beauty in blue, she's posing next to
my 1953 Kaiser Manhattan—the best car I ever had.

—Bob Crawford, Apple Valley, Minnesota

isn't it Romantic?

In the 1950s, pitching woo was different than it is today. But one thing's the same: Guys try to impress the object of their desire with a BNO—big night out.

Judy Goff of Chico, California enjoyed such a brush with high romance on New Year's Eve 1954. Her date, Larry Polson, took her to the then-renowned Papagallo Room in San Francisco's Fairmont Hotel.

"He was out to impress me," Judy recalls with a chuckle. "This guy had a little money. I was a bit out of my element. I remember having a nonalcoholic drink and a bacon-wrapped filet mignon for dinner, followed by a floor show, with a band and dancing. Most of all, I recall how special it was to be treated like an adult—to get a taste of what it would be like. I even was allowed to stay out until 1 a.m. instead of midnight for that one."

While the night was certainly memorable, Cupid made an early exit, Judy observes.

"I don't remember dating him after that," she says.

Sometimes, even the BNO isn't enough. But it sure is fun trying!

Turn the page for more love lessons....

Classicstock.com

VIVA Las Vegas!

THIS COUPLE ROLLED THE DICE AND GOT LUCKY IN LOVE.

By Marilyn Curtis, Pico Rivera, California

I won big in Las Vegas. No, not at the blackjack table or slot machine; I hit the jackpot when I wed my handsome groom, Earl, on July 21, 1951. Our wedding, at the Little Chapel of the West on the grounds of the Hotel Last Frontier, cost a mere $87 (less than our son Michael's tuxedo cost when he married in 1988).

I met Earl back in the summer of 1948, while vacationing in Los Angeles with friends. Minneapolis was my home; that's where I worked as a secretary for three executives at WCCO, a local radio station. One of my friends had previously worked with Earl, so he invited my husband-to-be out with us one evening. We had a great time, and even enjoyed a Sunday drive to Palm Springs the next day.

It wasn't until the following Tuesday that Earl and I had our first real date. He took me out to dinner and a movie. When we walked out of the theater, I turned to him and said, "That was a good movie, wasn't it?" He looked at me and replied, "I don't know. I was watching you the whole time." I still get choked up every time I think about it.

I thought Earl was a swell guy, but I had to return to Minneapolis for work. Shortly thereafter, however, Earl cleverly persuaded his folks to visit a cousin in St. Paul—a short drive from where I lived. Earl and I spent a few more days together and met each other's families.

For about a year, we kept our long-distance relationship alive through letters and phone calls. In August of 1949, I returned to Los Angeles to stay with his parents for a few days. That's where he pulled me into another room and said, "This is for you." In his outstretched hand was a beautiful engagement ring. Then he said, "This goes with it." He pulled out a box. Inside was a diamond wedding band.

Looking back, I realize he never asked if I would marry him, and I never said yes. I just put my hand out, and he slipped the beautiful ring on my finger.

After we got engaged, I lived in Minneapolis for another six months before moving out to Los Angeles. I loved my radio job. The work was always different and exciting. I used to tell Earl that he must »

SOUVENIR
from *Little Church* OF THE *West*
NEVADA'S FAMOUS CHAPEL ON THE DESERT

Hotel
LAST FRONTIER
LAS VEGAS, NEVADA

EARL + MARILYN CURTIS   7-21-51

have been pretty special for me to leave my job at the radio station. But it was worth it. I moved to California, got my own apartment and we set a wedding date.

Since my family and friends lived in Minnesota and Wisconsin and his brood in Omaha, we decided to keep it simple and exchange our vows in Vegas.

For months, I corresponded with the wedding director of the Hotel Last Frontier, managing to make all the arrangements in advance. The only snafu occurred when the director told me that the hotel was booked for the night. I was so disappointed. I mentioned it to my boss. He made one phone call and we got our room—it turned out he had a history of business dealings with the hotel. Lady Luck was already on our side!

In the meantime, I found my perfect wedding dress. Hanging in the window of a Huntington Park, California store, the ankle-length lace gown with matching jacket was beautiful. I hurried to my soon-to-be mother-in-law's house and we drove over together to see it. The price tag—$25!

Earl's folks and another couple who stood up for us accompanied us to Vegas. In the early '50s, the city was a far cry from the glittering light show it is today. There wasn't much traffic, and vast expanses of desert linked the handful of hotels and casinos that fronted the two-lane highway now known as the Las Vegas Strip.

After an intimate ceremony at the Little Church of the West, our party, still dressed to the nines, enjoyed an "expensive" dinner at the posh Flamingo Hotel. One of the most celebrated resorts of the time, it was built by mobster Benjamin "Bugsy" Siegel, a member of the Meyer Lansky crime organization. Dinner prices in the Flamingo Room ranged from $3.50 to $7.50.

During dinner, someone from our group must have told the band that we had tied the knot, because, to our surprise, Mr. Duke Ellington and his orchestra called us up on stage. They played *I Love You Truly*, and we

Price of love in the 1950s
Take a look at the Curtises' tab for their whirlwind wedding out west!

$25	Chapel charge, including flowers and candles, recorded music, the minister and four postcard wedding announcements (additional ones were 15 cents each)
$25	Wedding dress
$14	Bridal bouquet, two corsages and three boutonnieres
$10	Wedding photos, which included four poses (one 8×10 and six 5×7)
$8	One-night stay at the Hotel Last Frontier
$5	Marriage license
$87	**TOTAL!!**

danced in front of a room full of people. I couldn't tell you what a single person looked like; my eyes were fixed on Earl the entire time.

The next day we visited Hoover Dam, where we took an underground tour that revealed the inner workings of the power plant.

The following week, my folks hosted a reception in Minneapolis. Several old »

coworkers, friends and relatives came to wish us well. We left for California in Earl's '39 Chevy with a trunk jam-packed with wedding gifts.

When we crossed into the Golden State, a border guard stopped us to inspect our car. He opened the trunk, took a look at our stash and quickly closed it back up. He smiled, offered his best and sent us on our way.

I moved into the new three-bedroom, ranch-style home that Earl had built after a model he toured. It was part of a new subdivision in Pico Rivera, and, during construction, we would come out on weekends to watch the progress. In those times, we came to know everybody on the block.

Eleven years later, I became pregnant with our only son. I had waited so long for him that I wanted to be the one to raise him, so I retired after his birth to do so. He's 47 now and married, with a beautiful 15-year-old daughter of his own—named Savanna.

Now there are only four or so of us left from the original neighborhood. I'm proud to say that I've lived in this house for 58 years, and I never plan to move. There are just too many good memories that linger here.

Earl and I enjoyed 43 lovely years until his passing in 1994. Though Earl may be gone, I will always remember our life together. And, most certainly, our wonderful weekend wedding in the desert.

Rates and Information
Hotel
LAST FRONTIER
Las Vegas, Nevada

You'll Enjoy
The Early West in Modern Splendor
at the
HOTEL LAST FRONTIER

YOUR COMFORT. Entire hotel is air conditioned. 360 days of sunshine a year—delightfully cool nights. No fog.

YOUR MEALS. The choicest foods, prepared by experts, have given the Last Frontier a high reputation among gourmets.

YOUR ENTERTAINMENT. Every night in the big stone and log Ramona Room you may dance to the music of a nationally famous orchestra and enjoy a floor show featuring the top names of the entertainment world. Stars of stage, screen and radio headline the fine Ramona Room shows. No cover charge or minimum.

YOUR ACTIVE MOMENTS. There's a swimming pool, a stable with attendants and 30 horses, a pitch and putt golf course, croquet and badminton courts—all on the Hotel grounds. Fishing at Lake Mead and Colorado River, an hour away.

YOUR LEISURE. Two luxurious cocktail lounges—Gay 90's Bar and Carrillo Room. Gaming in the 21 Club Casino. Stage coach rides, barbecue parties.

LITTLE CHURCH OF THE WEST. Our wedding chapel, open 24 hours a day, is an exact replica, to half size of a pioneer gold rush town church.

FAMOUS LAST FRONTIER VILLAGE. Historic treasures of the Old West in an authentic restoration of a gold rush town. Free museum, collection of old vehicles, trains, guns, clocks, musical instruments—stores, shops, gambling hall and saloon, etc.

IN THE CENTER OF SCENIC AMERICA. Make this hotel your headquarters for visits to Hoover (Boulder) Dam, the Grand Canyon, Lake Mead, Zion National Park, Death Valley, Historic ghost towns. Transportation available.

HOW TO COME TO LAS VEGAS

BY AUTO. On U. S. Highway 91, 285 miles from Los Angeles. Also U. S. 93, connecting with U. S. 66 at Kingman, Arizona.

BY AIR. Served by Western Air Lines, United Air Lines, Trans World Air Lines and Bonanza Air Lines—1 hour and :5 minutes from Los Angeles.

BY TRAIN. On Union Pacific Main Line.

BY BUS. Transcontinental buses stop at our door.

ROOM RATES — ALL EUROPEAN PLAN

MAIN BUILDING

GUEST BEDROOM with tub and shower bath:

	Double Bed	Twin Bed
Single	$7.00	$7.00 - $8.00
Double	$8.00 - 9.00	$9.00 - 10 - 12

DELUXE BEDSITTING ROOM with tub and shower bath:

	Double Bed	Twin Bed
Single	$10.00	$11.00 - 12.00
Double	$12.00	$13.00 - 14.00

PENTHOUSE SUITE: DeLuxe Bedsitting Room, Private Bar, Boudoir, Tub and Shower Bath.

Single	$24
Double	$24

PATIO BUILDINGS

GUEST BEDROOM and bath:

Single	$5.00 - 6.00	$7.00
Double	$7.00 - 8.00	$7.00 - 9.00

(EXTRA PERSON IN ROOM - $1.50)

For reservations write, wire, teletype Las Vegas 8602 or phone at (Las Vegas 1800), see your travel agent—or consult our representatives—

GLEN W. FAWCETT ASSOCIATES
510 West Sixth Street
Los Angeles, California
Telephone: TRinity 3671

1114 Russ Building
San Francisco, California
Telephone: SUtter 1-5937

Who will provide direct teletype reservation service for you at no extra charge.

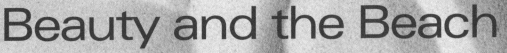

Beauty and the Beach

By Betty Frost, Coloma, Wisconsin

It was June 1953, and the thing to do on your day off was to go to Asbury Park and tan. My friend Joan Havas Lenker and I worked for the New Jersey Bell Telephone Co. in Mendham. I wore a new green bathing suit and carried a colorful beach bag.

Not long after we got set up for the day, a group of soldiers arrived; two came over and said they were going to photo school at Fort Monmouth and were assigned to take color pictures. One asked if I would pose for him. He was so polite, it didn't take long to say I would. He introduced himself: Jack Frost from Stevens Point, Wisconsin.

Two nights later he called and asked if he could come over with the pictures. We hit it off right away.

After many letters and four trips to Wisconsin when Jack was on leave, he was discharged and we were married in 1956. We moved down to the family farm in Coloma, and Jack started a game farm—Frost Waterfowl Trust. We were blessed with three children before Jack passed away in 1996.

But that green bathing suit was the best investment I ever made.

Remember Saying?

classy chassis
Female with a great figure

seeing stars

FROM THE SILVER SCREEN TO THE CONCERT STAGE, THESE CELEBRITIES MADE OUR PALMS SWEAT AND OUR PULSES RACE.

Marilyn Monroe. If this blond bombshell didn't make a man's pulse race, he needed a doctor. Monroe radiated an intoxicating blend of vulnerability and sensuality, combined with impeccable comic timing. Yet behind all that, the star of *Gentlemen Prefer Blondes* and *Some Like It Hot* also exuded a sense of melancholy that foreshadowed her death in 1962.

James Dean. A smoldering symbol of youthful rebellion, James Dean epitomized teenage cool—an image he honed in films like *East of Eden* and *Rebel Without a Cause*. Was there a cooler image than

Dean in a jean jacket, a cigarette dangling haphazardly from his lips? His bright career, however, was brief. His tragic death in a car accident at age 24 only solidified his live-fast, die-young legend.

Marlon Brando. Females swooned over this brooding hunk, who stormed to fame with a tour-de-force performance in *A Streetcar Named Desire*. He cemented his status as a superstar with equally mesmerizing roles in *The Wild One* and *On the Waterfront*, for which he won an Academy Award in 1954.

Elizabeth Taylor. This sensual starlet's life was the stuff of Hollywood legend. Taylor achieved super-celebrity status via blockbusters like *Cat on a Hot Tin Roof*, *Cleopatra*, *Butterfield 8* and *Who's Afraid of Virginia Woolf?* Eight marriages to celebrities like Eddie Fisher and Richard Burton, combined with a lifestyle as flamboyant as the diamonds she sports, only added luster.

Elvis Presley. Shown only from the waist up, Elvis the Pelvis nonetheless gyrated his way into America's homes in 1956 on *The Ed Sullivan Show*. An icon of American pop culture, the pouty-lipped Mississippi native sold millions of records and left many a female teen weak in the knees—and in the process revolutionized the music scene.

Marilyn Monroe

James Dean

boardwalk bike ride

I love this picture from 1953 of my friends Everett and Flossie enjoying a lovely day together in Ocean City.

— Leanne Flanagan
Fair Lawn, New Jersey

From 'Honey' to Honeymoon

By Elizabeth Grimes, Newnan, Georgia

My date, Don, came to pick me up in a gorgeous, classic red '57 Chevrolet convertible. We were planning to spend the day visiting friends who lived about a 3-hour drive away. The month was May, and the weather was warm. We had a lovely trip.

As we were leaving town, I said something to him and the word "Honey" slipped out. I looked to see if Don had noticed. But his expression didn't change, so I was relieved.

Two weeks later he was transferred to McChord AFB in Tacoma, Washington. We corresponded, and in his third letter he proposed, adding that he would not get much sleep until he heard from me. Not wanting to be the cause of sleepless nights, I sent him my answer.

The loudspeaker in his squadron building announced: "Lt. Grimes, you have a telegram." Don hurried over to get the telegram, which read: "The answer to your question is 'Yes'. I love you. Carol." When he looked up, everyone in the room was watching him. They had read it first!

A few weeks after we were married, he said, "You know when I knew you liked me? It was when we took that trip together and you called me 'Honey.'" I couldn't help but chuckle, and replied, "Sweetheart, don't you know that almost everybody calls everybody 'Honey' in the south?" But it was a sweet memory, and I'm glad now that I let the word slip out.

Revenge Is Sweet

By Dorothy Lott, Houston, Texas

In 1950, I worked for a telephone company, located in a building that also housed a light company and drugstore. One day a girl from the store told me that a fellow from the light company asked if she knew the black-haired girl who worked upstairs. She said she did, and he asked if she would ask if I would have a date with him. I told her I wouldn't go on a "date," but I would have a Coke with him.

Some time after that Coke, he asked if we could double-date with another couple. I agreed.

The first Sunday in June was "splash day," a day when young folks headed for Ratcliff Lake, a half-hour drive from Lufkin, Texas, where I lived.

I was in my new sundress, sitting on the front porch swing and waiting for him to pick me up, when he called. He said he had car trouble and added that if he was not at the lake in an hour, he would just see me at church that night.

I was fuming when a neighbor boy drove up and asked me what I was doing. I told him I would know soon, so he joined me on the swing. When a half-hour went by, I leaped up and said, "I'm going to Ratcliff Lake with you!" He just about fainted. He had been trying to date me for some time.

Soon after we arrived, my eye fell on a boat with four people in it—one of whom looked like my suitor. Suddenly, I noticed the boat retreating. Sure enough, all four of them abandoned the boat and climbed into a little green Chevy and took off.

On the ride home I imagine my date was trying to figure out what was bugging me. The truth was that I was planning James William Lott's demise.

That afternoon, I rode to church with my parents but instead of going in I sat outside, waiting for him. When he and his friends arrived, I made them all sit in the first row with me.

Later, as we drove to a drive-in, the silence was deafening. I asked casually, "Well, what did you all do today?" The other couple didn't say a word, and Jim stammered something about being stuck at home all afternoon. I said, "Well, I had a most interesting and exciting day—I went to Ratcliff Lake!" Silence. Then, "So that was you!" I said, "Yeah, that was me, and now this 'date' is over!"

The next morning, my telephone started ringing and didn't stop. Persistence paid off, I guess. I told everybody that I had decided I was going to make him pay for the rest of his life.

So I married him 6 months later. That was almost 57 years ago. He's still paying!

wedding day bliss

Here's a picture of my groom, James, and I as we opened our gifts on our August 1955 wedding day in Walworth, New York. Advertised by the manufacturer in 1952 as "the perfect gift," we enjoyed our Universal Coffeematic coffeemaker for years.

— *Janice Wignal Mitchell, Colorado Springs, Colorado*

'50s Dating for Dummies

The 1950s ushered in a new age of dating as the first baby boomers—granted more freedom than any previous generation—hit their teen years.

Back then, dating had its own set of social rituals, including many that seem hopelessly quaint by today's standards. Here's a look back at some dos and don'ts that show why spending a Saturday night with your sweetheart during the Eisenhower era was the cat's meow.

Dating etiquette for girls:
* Only floozies ask guys out.
* When someone asks you out, it's polite to give an immediate answer.
* Never break a date without providing a valid reason.
* There's no such thing as fashionably late; be ready when your date arrives.
* It's only proper to introduce your date to your parents.

Pictorial Press Ltd./Alamy

* Don't apply makeup in public (please see first point).
* At a restaurant, it's ladylike to tell a date what you want for dinner, so he can order for you.
* Don't humiliate guys by trying to pay for a date.

Dating etiquette for guys:
* Dates aren't like cramming for exams; don't wait until the last minute to ask a girl out.
* It's poor form to honk the car horn to announce your arrival; call for her at the door.
* Ask her parents when they want her home—and make sure your watch works.
* It's only polite to help her don her coat.
* Real gentlemen open car doors for girls—or any door, for that matter.
* It's chivalrous to walk between her and the curb.
* Bring enough money along.
* No kissing on the first date.
* On prom night, don't leave the corsage in the fridge.

journal entry

my best (and worst!) date ever!

ocean voyages of fate

By Rose Merola Squitieri, Bayonne, New Jersey

He fell in love with a photograph of me, and that's how it all started.

The bearer of that photograph was my brother. He had been in the service and, while on furlough in Italy, visited a family friend, Luigi Squitieri, where he shared some family pictures, including one of me.

Two years later, Luigi came to America to meet the girl in the photograph. Seemingly pleased, he said, "So this is Rose."

The next day, he visited with my parents. We sat in the yard, where he told me that when he had seen the picture, he vowed then that he would come to America to meet "that girl" and marry her.

I was 33; he was 40. Neither of us had been married. A few months later, on Oct. 1, 1955, we left for Europe on the luxury liner

"He fell in love with a photograph of me, and that's how it all started."

Andrea Doria. We arrived in Naples 8 days later, and on Oct. 31, 1955, on a sunny Monday morning, we were married in St. Peter's Cathedral in Rome.

The next year, we made the decision to return to the United States, where Luigi would become a permanent citizen. I would go first and he would follow after selling his condominium in Rome.

In the meantime, he booked passage on

the *Andrea Doria* to arrive in America on July 26. Our son was born on July 22. During this time, I persuaded Luigi to postpone the voyage until the condo sale was in order.

Had my husband not heeded my advice, he may never have seen our firstborn.

In the now-famous incident near Nantucket, Massachusetts, the *Andrea Doria* collided with another ocean liner, the *Stockholm*, on the night of July 25 and went down July 26—the day it was supposed to have arrived with my beloved.

Luigi booked passage on the *Cristoforo Colombo* and arrived in time for our son's christening on Sept. 9. Our daughter was born 21 months later. We had a marriage that lasted 33 beautiful years.

Only God knows if I saved my husband's life by persuading him to postpone his trip, but certainly it was not without His help.

Saturday Evening Post, circa 1959

130

Marriage Made in the Reed Section

By Harold Kohn, Columbus, Ohio

Oak Ridge, Tennessee, the home of the Oak Ridge National Laboratory, was a small town where all the single people knew each other.

So when a new girl or guy arrived, there was a flurry of activity. That was the case one day in 1956 as I was attending a seminar in the auditorium.

A new girl rushed in at the last minute, looking great. Fortunately, her picture appeared in the next issue of *Lab News*. She was Janet Mitchell, 22, a recent graduate of the University of California.

In my teen years, I'd worked as a process server and had learned to track people down. So I did some sleuthing and managed to find Janet's apartment building and telephone number. Much to my surprise, she said yes to a blind date.

When Janet opened the door to greet me, there stood the smallest, baldest and oldest man she'd ever go out with. On top of that, my car was a tiny British Hillman Husky with virtually no springs or shocks, and we traveled 19 miles over some of the worst roads in east Tennessee.

But I behaved well at the restaurant, didn't handle my silverware like a Neanderthal and took her to a concert. There I sensed Janet had played a musical instrument before.

When she confirmed she'd played the saxophone in high school and clarinet in college, I asked if she'd like to learn how to play the bassoon.

Our local symphony orchestra owned a bassoon in the hopes some hapless person would appear to play it. Janet agreed to try, and, before long, we were playing together in the orchestra and dating.

We've made beautiful music together ever since.

love songs of the '50s

Whether making out or making up, these are the ballads that made us weak in the knees.

Love Letters in the Sand
— *Pat Boone*

Love Me Tender
— *Elvis Presley*

Young Love
— *Sonny James*

Love Is a Many-Splendored Thing
— *The Four Aces*

All I Have to Do Is Dream
— *The Everly Brothers*

Venus
— *Frankie Avalon*

I Only Have Eyes for You
— *The Flamingos*

Secret Love
— *Doris Day*

On the Street Where You Live
— *Vic Damone*

Since I Don't Have You
— *The Skyliners*

Kisses Sweeter Than Wine
— *Jimmie Rodgers*

Tonight You Belong to Me
— *Patience and Prudence*

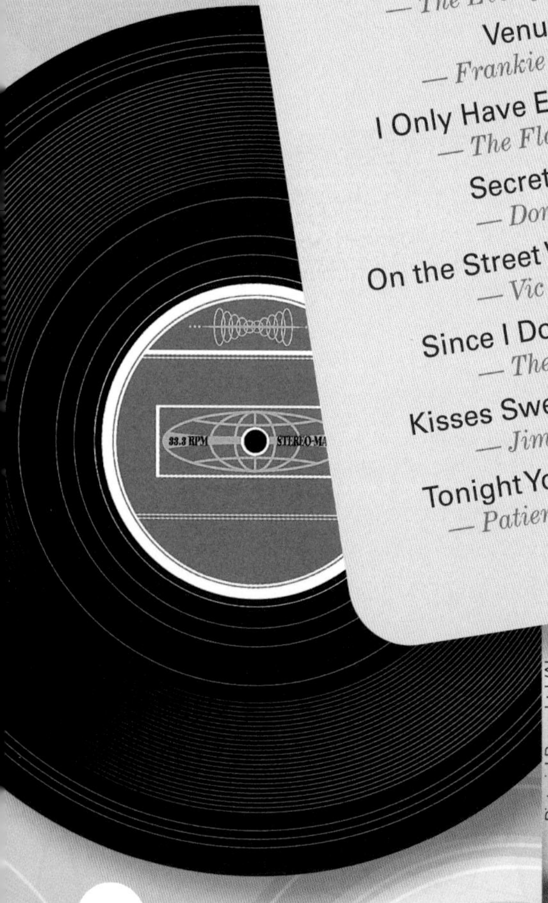

Stockbyte/Superstock

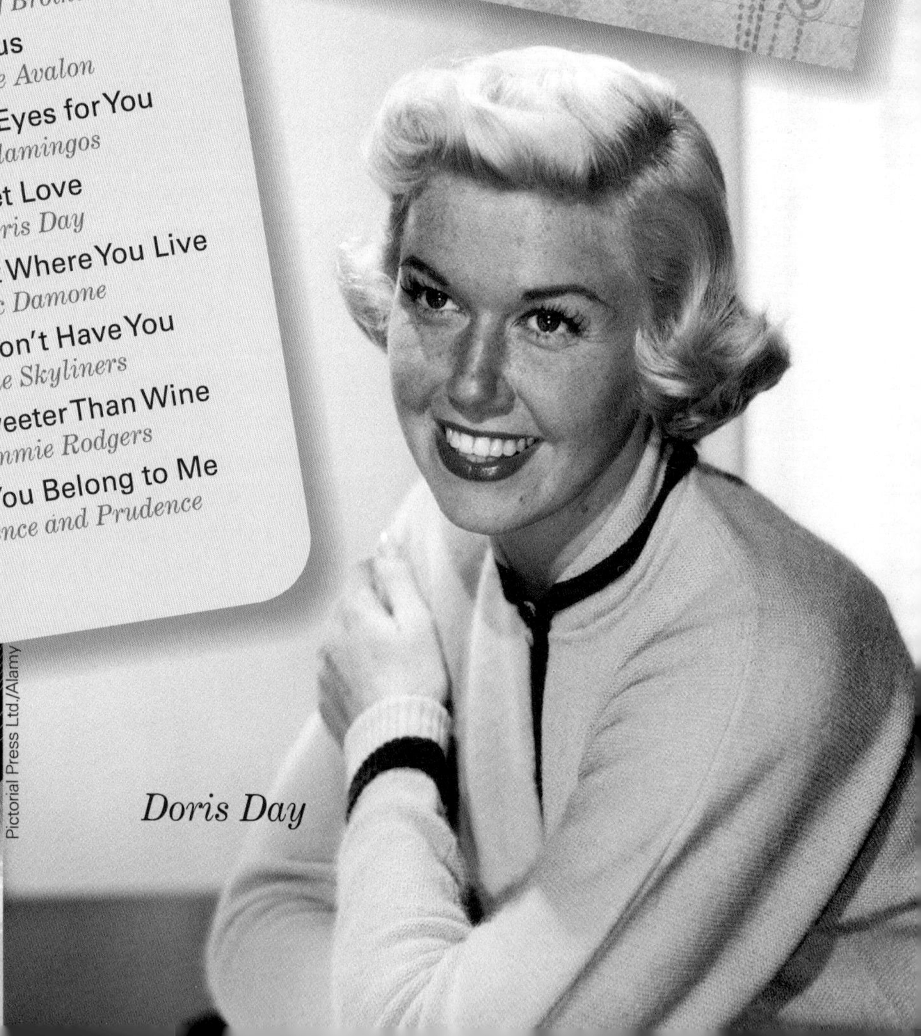

Pictorial Press Ltd./Alamy

Doris Day

happy trails

By Peg Hevel, Salmon, Idaho

One evening, while a camp nurse at the YMCA of the Rockies in Colorado, I removed a large splinter from a man's arm. During the procedure, he asked about a date. I thought, *How can I graciously say no?*

Just then, the clinic door opened. My mind whispered, *It's the Marlboro cowboy right out of the ad!* His slender frame filled out his Levi's jeans. The heels of his Tony Lama boots were worn on the edges. The brim of his tan Western hat sat snug above brown eyes.

He smiled, held out a couple of syringes and needles and asked, "Would you sterilize these for me? I have a horse that needs penicillin for a wire-cut infection."

"I'll be right with you," I said.

"So," my patient said, "Will you go out with me tonight?"

"Sorry, she has a date with me," the cowboy said.

I smiled, saying, "Yes, I do."

After the patient left, the cowboy said, "I'm Don Hevel."

I introduced myself and said, "Thank you for saving me from an awkward situation."

"No problem," he said, adding, "Can I buy you a cup of coffee?"

That was the start of over 47 years of rainbow-colored adventures with my "Marlboro cowboy."

When the steam swirls over my morning coffee, I feel a hug to my heart and a whispered memory: *Can I buy you a cup of coffee?* I look at my cowboy and smile.

circa 1950

Beryl and Harry Riley, 1954

coffee catastrophe

By Beryl Riley, Highspire, Pennsylvania

I met my American husband, Harry, while he was stationed at Bushy Park in Teddington, Middlesex in England from 1951 to 1955.

We married on Oct. 16, 1954, and went on a week's honeymoon in a town called Eastbourne. When we returned to our small apartment, it was my 21st birthday and I was ready to try my hand at housewifery by making him our very first breakfast together at home.

I had very little cooking experience but went all out and made him eggs, bacon, fried tomatoes and toast.

Everything was going well…until I made the coffee. Coffee was nowhere near as popular as it is today, and I had grown up drinking tea, England's national drink. So Harry had to show me how to use a coffeepot.

A short while later, I called him to the table for a lovely breakfast. Impressed, he sat down and I proudly proceeded to finish things off by pouring a fresh cup of coffee. But when I tipped the pot, only hot water filled his mug! My dear husband looked at me strangely and put the pot back on the stove. I had no idea that the coffee needed time to perk.

We eventually enjoyed (and I learned to make) a good cup of coffee—a "perk" that we shared the 45 years we spent together.

The Farmer Takes a Wife

By Mary Kershner, Findlay, Ohio

Howard and I had a blind date on May 6, 1951, and liked each other from the start. By the spring of 1952, we were sure we wanted to get married.

In May, Howard's mother wrote to the *Bride and Groom* TV show in hopes that we could get married on the air. Howard's father was sick and couldn't leave the house for our wedding, but he could see it if we got married on television.

In July, Howard received a letter and application form with questions about how we met, where we went on dates and our likes and dislikes.

At the end of August, we received a telegram saying we'd be on *Bride and Groom* Oct. 1! Howard was the first farmer who'd ever applied, and that was one reason we were chosen.

A month later, around the time of my 20th birthday, we were on our way to New York City.

When we arrived, we toured the TV studio, met everyone connected with the program and got our marriage license. We had rehearsals, and I was fitted for a beautiful wedding gown from the show's wardrobe department.

Then came the big day. We got into our wedding clothes and makeup; it was time for us to get married! The ceremony ran from noon to 12:15, including the commercials, and was sponsored by Betty Crocker.

Mary and Howard Kershner, *Bride and Groom*, 1952

Afterward, we received our gifts—two pieces of farm machinery, wedding rings, luggage, a stove, silverware, an iron and a toaster. Then we were given a rental car and sent on our wedding trip—a 5-night, all-expenses-paid stay at Hidden Valley Ranch near Lake Luzerne, New York.

Because our wedding was televised, most of the people in our hometowns were able to see it. Those who didn't have televisions went to stores that sold them so they could watch. Even the furniture store where my dad worked closed down that day so that he and his coworkers could witness the event.

love on the rocks

By Walter C. Ball, Walnut Creek, California

In the summer of 1954, a friend suggested that I try the 6-day saddle trip from Yosemite Valley to the High Sierra Camps. On the first day, I arrived at the stables and was greeted by the guide, who introduced me to the only other rider who had already arrived. "Mr. Ball, this is LuAlice Dunahee. You'll be spending the next 6 days together." Little did I know that it was only the beginning of an incredible journey together!

Our trip was beautiful. We shared breathtaking views of clear lakes, powerful waterfalls, towering granite cliffs, snow-capped mountains and more. But as we traveled, LuAlice and I discovered we had many things in common, from enjoying similar music to sharing the same values.

When our group returned to Yosemite

Valley, I took her out to dinner. Afterward, we watched the incredible "Firefall," a twilight bonfire pushed slowly over the edge of a cliff. We held hands and listened to the romantic strains of *Indian Love Call* playing in the background as the fiery sparks swirled.

I guess it was appropriate that we met in such a rocky location, because it seems our fate was set in stone. Though we lived some 400 miles apart, after 13 months of trading letters, tape recordings and visits, we were married in 1955.

first kiss

Bruce Thompson of Waukesha, Wisconsin shares this photograph of his son Steve enjoying his first kiss with the girl next door in 1954. It just goes to show that young love can't be fenced in.

can-do America

In the early 1950s, the odds of John Marchese holding a job were as solid as the wooden pins he hand-set at a local bowling alley for 10 cents a line.

"Unemployment was not an option," says Marchese, who grew up in Milwaukee, Wisconsin. "My parents wanted me to be productive and thrifty—to understand the value of a dollar. My sisters and I were very proud about having savings accounts."

As a pinsetter, Marchese earned $2 to $3 a shift on Friday and Saturday nights. The work—a frantic race to set up fallen pins and return bowling balls on two adjacent lanes—was intense.

"You hoped to see some gutter balls," he says with a chuckle. "Every so often, someone would buy me a Coke or slide a quarter down the lane to me for a tip."

To earn more dough, Marchese also delivered newspapers from a coaster wagon, earning $4.70 a week. He also earned a priceless bonus: a can-do work ethic that helped him convert the 7-10 splits of life.

Here are more stories about the hardworking people who helped make this country great....

The Girls in Blue

SPECIAL SERVICES WAS A WELCOME RESPITE FOR GIs.

By Saralou Caliri, Southern Pines, North Carolina

They called us "the girls in blue" or DACs—for Department of Army Civilians under Army Special Services. We weren't the Red Cross, the USO or the military. We were recreation directors in service clubs, which were off-duty centers on Army posts for enlisted personnel.

Our job was to provide a convenient place for enlisted men to relax when off duty. We used to joke that our job was to "keep the boys off the streets."

I took this very seriously, getting one of them off the streets and keeping him. I met David in Straubing, Germany in 1956, and we've been married since 1958.

Ideally, service clubs had a lounge for reading, playing cards or writing letters and an area for evening programs. We held talent shows, dances, card tournaments and whatever else we could dream up.

Sometimes the service club had a library, craft shop, photo lab or musical instruments. Some clubs were small one-room sites.

I'm not sure the Service Club branch of Special Services even exists anymore. But during the Korean War it played an important role in the lives of military men and women, providing a home away from home and contact with caring people.

I was fortunate enough to have been assigned to Japan, Korea and Germany in my 6 years of service. Being in Special Services was sort of a two-way ministry. I often thought we should have been a branch of the Chaplain's Office.

ODDS GOOD IN KOREA

When I first went to Korea, I was assigned to Koje, an island off the southeastern tip of the country, with 10,000 men and six of us women.

Our living quarters became known as "the black shack" because it was a shack with a black tar-paper roof. Our rooms were connected to a common room with a potbellied stove as the only source of heat. There were other residents, too—one night I woke up as a rat ran across my face.

We were important to the men stationed there for many reasons. We were women and reminded them of their other, better lives. We were good listeners. And at the club we were there strictly for enlisted personnel, without any interference from officers.

On our own time, however, we could eat and socialize anywhere on the post—at the officers' club or mess, the NCO club or mess or the enlisted men's club or mess. We were treated as friends, respected and looked after. Never were so few taken care of by so many!

A later assignment took me to the camp of the UN Armistice Commission near Panmunjom. When I arrived, I was the only woman and had to stay at another post nearby.

A helicopter was sent each morning to »

BOATING AND DANCING. Tours were a fun club activity, including this one by boat.

SERVICE WITH A SMILE. Saralou helped soldiers spend their time off at this building, called the Willow Service Club.

DIM THE LIGHTS. A scene from the "Willow Service Club presents *South Pacific*" production.

DEALING AND CUTTING. That's David, Saralou's future husband (sitting at the front table, facing the camera), at the bridge table in the card room.

BLANCHE IN A BUG. Saralou's friend—and now *Reminisce* staffer—Blanche Freischle Comiskey was also a "girl in blue" with Saralou at the Willow Service Club.

'All right, guys, listen up!' he'd yell. 'There's a woman present, so...act like gentlemen, if you can remember how!'

take me to work. Next to the service club was a theater. Whenever I wanted to see a movie, I stopped at the entrance and called for the sergeant in charge so he could go in and announce my presence.

"All right, guys, listen up!" he'd yell. "There's a woman present, so can the comments, the hoots and hollers and act like gentlemen, if you can remember how!"

Later, when there were two women at the service club, the same sergeant would send a couple of guys ahead of us to clear the shower when it was our turn, then stand guard.

One of the most special places I was assigned was Straubing, on the site of a former German Luftwaffe officers' candidate school.

It was the most picturesque Army site I've ever seen. Permanent Bavarian-style buildings with trees, grass, flowers and a pool made it look more like a college campus or country club than a military base.

Our club was called the Willow Service Club because of the huge willow trees draped over the side patio. It was here that I met my husband and also a co-worker named Blanche Freischle, now Blanche Comiskey.

AN ENCHANTED EVENING

While at Straubing, someone suggested we put on the musical *South Pacific*.

The next thing I knew, we were knee-deep in planning and seeking rights for the play.

It must have been destiny, because we had nearly all the ingredients right there—the 83rd Army Band, talented soldiers and Army wives, including a Mary Martin look-alike who had seen the Broadway production.

We scrounged naval uniforms from Bremerhaven and recruited the string section from the local orchestra in town. Blanche even found someone to build us the famous *I'm Gonna Wash That Man Right Outa My Hair* shower.

With the rehearsal running quite late, we were all exhausted and cranky. The snack bar stayed open for us until after rehearsal, and the cast went ahead while I took care of some things.

When I finally arrived, everyone stood up and broke into song with *There Is Nothing Like...Saralou!*

Is it any wonder I look on my years with Special Services as a special time in my life?

Writing Assignment

By Lewis Lowe, Sumter, South Carolina

In 1956 I was stationed at Sembach Air Force Base in Germany. I was the only one in the squadron who had a car, so naturally I had a lot of friends. In our free time, we would sightsee and just do what guys do.

One day the first sergeant called me into his office and handed me a letter. It read, "Dear Sir, I have a son in your command that I have not heard from in several months. Please advise me of his whereabouts."

The first sergeant sent me to my room to grab pen and paper, then made me sit in his office and write my father a letter. I assumed my assignment was over, until he said he would see me tomorrow at the same time.

After 3 weeks of writing to my father, I asked if I could write my sister. He informed me that I could…on my own time.

KOS/Alamy

home from the sea

My brother, Bobby Oncin, was home on leave on this day in 1957. He and my husband, Bill, posed in front of our Oldsmobile outside our home in Rosedale, New York.
—Odette Landers
Fort Pierce, Florida

medal mix-up

By H. Vincent Peffley, Ottawa, Illinois

While stationed in Argentia, Newfoundland with the Navy Seabees in 1956, I was awarded a Good Conduct medal for completed service.

I wrote my wife a letter with a full explanation and packaged the medal separately. They were mailed at the same time, but the medal arrived first.

The purple ribbon, to her, could only mean a Purple Heart medal for sure. She began to wonder what had happened to her husband in far-off Newfoundland.

Relief came with the arrival of my letter. But she had a few days of real concern!

strange bedfellows

By Richard McCarthy, Gleason, Wisconsin

For 4 to 6 weeks in the spring of 1953, a 6-1/2-foot-tall bunker in Korea was home to the communications section of Fox Co. 2nd Battalion, 1st Marines, 1st Marine Division.

Four of us—Michael "Miggs" Miggalousi, Tommy Laughlin, June "Willie" Williams and I—were the "comm," short for the communications unit.

We painted up signs that read "Home Sweet Home" and "Our Home," along with our names—a joke, since we were in a combat zone.

Though we didn't have many visitors, we did have some regular houseguests that took our sign seriously—four or five rats. They would run across our bellies when we tried to sleep!

Luckily for us, our visitors were never more than a nuisance, and I don't recall any of us getting bitten. Still, I'll never forget those weeks in our makeshift home away from home.

men in uniform

My buddies and I were just about to be mustered out of the service when we were photographed in September 1956 in Carmel, California. I'm on the far right. I served for 3 years, from 1953 to 1956, most of the time in Germany. I was a medic with the 5th Infantry Division. When I returned, I spent the last 4 months at Fort Ord in California and taught first-aid classes. I was taking a break after class when the other slide of me in my uniform was taken.

—*John Rusnak, Oak Lawn, Illinois*

a photographic memory

By Heyward Hoover, Centerville, Georgia

When I was 17, I was a fan of World War II hero General Dwight D. Eisenhower. One day in 1952, while he was campaigning in Columbia, South Carolina, my scoutmaster called me out of school.

As it turned out, he needed Eagle Scouts to flank both sides of a staircase on the state capitol as Ike left after meeting with the governor, James F. Byrnes. So 13 other scouts and I lined up on the stairs.

As confetti and balloons floated from rooftops, newsreel cameramen started grinding and more than 100 print reporters stood poised with notebooks and pencils. Cameramen jockeyed for good viewing angles, and radio reporters strategically positioned their microphones. Then Ike appeared on the statehouse steps with Byrnes.

As Ike came down the stairs, I wanted to shake this great man's hand. So I leaned over and stuck out my hand. He graciously stopped, clasped it tightly and shook. I didn't wash it for the rest of the week.

High-Flying Career Woman

By Betty Rollison, Roseville, California

The two years that I was a full-time hostess for Trans World Airlines in the early 1950s were two of the best years of my life!

While other airlines used the term "stewardess," TWA chose the title "hostess." It was hoped that the name would have a soothing effect on potential customers. Hostesses were expected to treat passengers as they would treat guests in their own homes.

To become a hostess, a woman had to be unmarried and meet certain requirements with regard to age, height, weight, appearance and attitude. In the early days of air travel, hostesses had to be registered nurses to assure novice passengers that personal care was the airline's primary aim.

At the time, TWA was the No. 1 airline for movie stars. We were informed when anyone of importance was onboard one of our flights. Among the celebrities on my flights were George Jessel and the Andrews Sisters.

During my time as a hostess, I met and fell in love with a crew member. My future husband was originally hired as a flight engineer and later became co-pilot and then captain. When we married, I had to resign. I was making $200 a month at the time.

I still meet socially with former flight attendants from TWA and other airlines, who flew in the era I did. We share stories and recall the fun we had when being a "hostess" was our full-time job.

TRAINED FOR TWA. To mark their graduation from TWA's 4-week training course, hostesses had a souvenir photo taken Dec. 12, 1952, at Kansas City Airport in Kansas City, Missouri. Author Betty (Sutherland) Rollison is the eighth person from the right. Behind the women is the Martin 404, with the Constellation in the background.

journal entry

my best (and worst) job!

In a Man's World

By Ruth Fenton, Venice, Florida

In 1943 I found myself working as a home economist for the Westinghouse Corporation.

As I demonstrated washers, dryers and stoves, I watched the salesmen and thought, "I could do that." So one day I approached a sales executive to try to convince him I could sell appliances as well as the men.

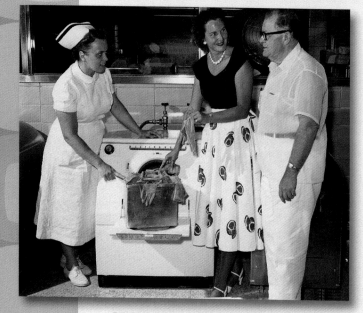

COMING CLEAN. In 1955, Ruth showed a nurse and doctor at Chicago's Cook County Hospital that a Westinghouse washer could clean their rubber gloves.

He was reluctant at first but finally decided to give me a chance. Soon I was outselling the men and was promoted to district sales representative—the first woman in Westinghouse to hold that position.

As Chicago territory manager, I became the only female, wholesale, major-appliance salesperson in the '50s at Westinghouse.

I loved the challenge of selling, especially because that was where the money was. I believe I had an edge because I had demonstrated products for buyers earlier on their floors, so they already knew me.

The first time I called on one buyer, he exploded at me for some reason. I was so nervous I couldn't remember prices or model numbers. I was about to burst into tears, so I excused myself. Later I learned some of the salesmen had seen my red eyes and complained to the buyer about his behavior. The next time I saw that buyer, he was quite gentle, though he told me I had to have broad shoulders if I was going to call on him.

Because I was working in a male world, there were some awkward moments. At meetings with other territory managers, they usually guessed I was a secretary. When I told them I was a TM, they looked astonished!

I went to one meeting for 150 TMs where the first speaker welcomed us, then said, "I was going to tell you a story, but I see there's a woman present." I felt like crawling into my shell!

A company newsletter once ran a story about me with the headline: "It's a TM. It's a Leader in Sales. It's a WOMAN!"

One of my biggest problems was taking businessmen to lunch. They always wanted to pick up the check, but I realized letting them do it would be a big mistake. Eventually I began telling them before we left for the restaurant that the entire meal was on Westinghouse.

After I left Westinghouse Corporation, I sold real estate in Florida and was very successful. Family members always joked that everything I touched turned to gold. But I loved my career and the challenge of competing in what was at the time definitely a man's game.

Dial telephone equipment for Bell System getting final check at a Western Electric factory.

BUSY... *behind the lines*

TODAY, telephone lines are defense lines. We're hard at work making more telephone equipment to carry the calls that speed America's production, direct civilian defense, and guide the Armed Forces.

ONE BIG REASON why America has dependable telephone service today is that Western Electric, the manufacturing unit of the Bell System, has

worked hand in hand over the years with Bell Telephone Laboratories who design the equipment and the telephone companies who operate it.

IN ADDITION, we're busily applying our long Bell System experience to making special electronic and communications equipment needed by the Armed Forces for the protection of this country.

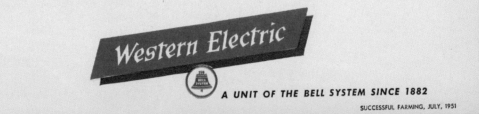

A UNIT OF THE BELL SYSTEM SINCE 1882

SUCCESSFUL FARMING, JULY, 1951

30

Successful Farming, circa 1951

Incredible Edibles

By Elaine Ferency Guzik, Detroit, Michigan

The 1950s were gastronomical heaven to me! Our family lived in a two-story, two-bedroom house attached to the back of Ferency's Market in a largely Hungarian neighborhood of southwest Detroit called Delray. When my father returned from World War II, he became the proprietor of the store—as was his father before him.

Food was plentiful. We never ran out of milk or had to go to the supermarket for missing ingredients. Our meat man, who was also my godfather, delivered sides of beef or pork, hams and lunch meats weekly. The Farm Crest bread man and the Twin Pines milkman delivered fresh bread and doughnuts or dairy products every other day.

Ferency's kolbasz (Hungarian sausage) was well-known and made weekly in a 5-foot-high, cast-iron sausage machine in the basement. Dad's meat and spice mixture was blended in a tub, then loaded into the top of the machine. Once the salt-encrusted sheep casings were rinsed and attached to the nozzle, a large hand-crank was turned, filling large metal pans with lengths of aromatic sausage. Half the sausage would be strung on poles in the smokehouse behind the house, sending the aroma of spicy meat wafting through the neighborhood.

Two blocks away was the poultry store. Dad would choose live chickens to be taken to the back room and "prepped" for selling.

Less than a half-mile from home, the produce terminal occupied two city blocks. We'd drive our "woody" station wagon there and load it up with eggs, fruits and vegetables from the vendors.

When my brothers and I were deemed responsible enough, we were allowed to scoop and measure packages of lard from metal tins, arrange produce displays, stock shelves, deliver groceries to the elderly, stamp price labels on goods, scrub the butcher block with a wire brush, help make the sausage, scrub pigs' feet to sell, work the old cash register and pack groceries.

During store hours, Dad was always in "uniform"—white shirt, bow tie usually created by Mom, and white butcher apron.

Eventually, supermarkets that could buy in volume and offer discount prices moved into the area, and the little mom-and-pop grocery stores like ours went out of business. But what a delicious world we grew up in!

Driving Mr. Truman

By La Monte C. Harris
Shawnee Mission, Kansas

While driving a Yellow Cab in Kansas City, Missouri in the fall of 1954, I had an unexpected fare. I was waiting for the light to change at 10th and Grand when a gentleman got into the backseat of my taxi. He requested I take him to the Kansas City Club and let him out at the side entrance.

As I turned north on Grand, I noticed who my passenger was—none other than former President Harry Truman. My wife says it's a wonder I didn't run up on the sidewalk. I calmly made the observation that my passenger bore a striking resemblance to President Truman. He replied, "That's not unusual, because I am Harry Truman."

When we reached the side entrance of the Kansas City Club, he left my cab. As he got out, three young men from a Future Farmers of America convention came down the sidewalk toward us. One of them said, "Hey, that's President Truman!" But by that time, Mr. Truman was already inside.

I still find it hard to believe that I talked one-on-one with the former president. And as for the tip he gave me, I should have kept it for posterity. It was all of 25 cents.

C Walter Bibikow/DanitaDelimont.com

Remember Saying?

boss

Great

Tied to Tobacco

By Helen Price Raper, Rocky Mount, North Carolina

Summers were hot and dirty on our family's tobacco farm in Battleboro, North Carolina in the '50s. Tobacco was the chief cash crop in eastern North Carolina, and "putting in"—as tobacco harvesting was called—was a big part of our lives.

The harvest season lasted from about July 1st until late fall. We usually worked 6 days a week, but never on the Sabbath.

At harvest time, at least three or four men spent their days out in the field pulling the tobacco leaves from the plants. Six to eight of us worked together, transferring these leaves to a bench and tying them to sticks.

The sticks were hung in the tobacco barn where the leaves were cured—heated until they were completely dried—for about a week. Then we helped remove the dried leaves from the sticks before they could be taken to the warehouse to be sold and turned into cigarettes and smoking tobacco.

With five boys and five girls in our family, Daddy always had help. We'd start when we were about 8 years old and work every summer until we got married and left home.

It was hard work, but, back then, neighbor helped neighbor and relative helped relative. Regardless, we could always have fun and cut a watermelon or two for a sweet, juicy reward.

Did You Know?
The average annual income in 1953 was $4,706. Minimum wage was paid at 75 cents an hour!

evening news

Green eyeshades, typewriters, scissors and paste pots. Ashtrays. Oh, how the newsrooms of yesterday differ from those of today. This photo from 1952 shows the newsroom at the Newark Evening News in Newark, New Jersey, on Market Street. "Pictured is only a fraction of the large staff, including yours truly," reports Doug McClelland of Neptune, New Jersey. "I'm standing in the back, turned to the camera, wearing a white shirt and bow tie and looking like Jimmy Olsen, cub reporter."

CHAPTER EIGHT

holidays & Celebrations

During the '50s in Jericho, New York, flicks and fireworks were a Fourth of July staple—right up there with hot dogs and apple pie.

"On the Fourth, we'd go to the drive-in for a double feature and watch fireworks between movies," recalls Joanne Weintraub of Milwaukee, Wisconsin. "It wasn't a huge display, but for a small town on Long Island, it was very cool."

During the first movie, Weintraub and her sister, Donna, would curl up with pillows in the backseat of their dad's white 1957 Chevrolet Impala. Instead of buying popcorn, her parents would bring a tasty treat: Kool-Aid and marshmallows covered with toasted coconut. After the fireworks, it was time for a snooze.

"I never saw a complete second feature," she says, chuckling.

Weintraub's family frequented the drive-in because it was much more economical than a movie theater.

"On the Fourth of July, there was nowhere else in the world I would've rather been," she says.

Read on and remember how we marked the year's most special days....

Aunt Agnes and the Easter Dresses

WITH A PHONE CALL, THIS READER PROVES THAT IT'S NEVER TOO LATE TO OFFER SIMPLE THANKS FOR A BOUQUET OF SPRINGTIME BLESSINGS.

By Charlene Derby, Santa Ana, California

My two sisters and I grew up near Bronson, Michigan. We lived in the country, the perfect backdrop for my favorite time of the year—spring.

I loved the warm spring rain showers that coaxed the crocuses from the ground, and I eagerly participated in the plans for Easter dinner.

But most of all, I looked forward to the package from Aunt Agnes that arrived about a week before Easter. My sisters and I knew it contained our Easter dresses.

Rose Mary, Millie and I were "stair-step" sisters, with Rose Mary the oldest and me in the middle. That meant Millie and I wore a lot of hand-me-down clothes. Flour-sack slips were also the norm.

So when the new dresses from Aunt Agnes arrived, they brightened our spring like the returning sunshine.

Aunt Agnes Lombard was our dad's sister. She was an unmarried career woman who lived about 300 miles away in Petoskey and served as both a benefactor and mentor to

her nieces.

The first Easter outfits from her that I remember were the sailor dresses we received in 1955. Mine was a sunny-yellow stripe, Rose Mary's a marine blue and Millie's a peony pink. On Easter Sunday, we sailed into church looking like triplets.

Aunt Agnes often visited us for Easter dinner and usually took pictures of us in our new outfits.

"You look as fresh as a spring breeze," she'd say.

In the spring of 1957, Aunt Agnes bought us pretty pastel cotton dresses for Easter. They weren't identical, but each had a special feature.

My lavender dress had a row of buttons across the bodice. Rose Mary's blue dress had a half-vest of cotton lace, while Millie's pale-yellow dress was trimmed with a black velvet ribbon.

We looked like a spring bouquet of lilac, iris and daffodil as we headed for church.

These dresses were also practical enough to wear to school. I wore mine once a week, »

EASTER TRADITION. Charlene Derby finally formally thanked her aunt Agnes (opposite page) for the Easter dresses the three nieces received every year. The girls showed off their frocks in 1955 (top), 1959 (below) and 1957 (right). Charlene is in the middle in the top photo.

even if Mom didn't have the time to iron it.

Then, in 1959, Aunt Agnes brought us into the world of high fashion with blue linen suits. With their crisp white collars and cuffs and gold-tone buttons, we looked ready for a parade.

The suits came with matching hats and purses that we used to carry our Sunday school offerings.

Aunt Agnes was there with her camera when it was time for church. She said we looked lovelier than a row of bluebells in a country lane.

Those suits became our standard Sunday attire until the jackets lost their shape and the buttons lost their shine.

As we grew into teenagers and started high school, my sisters and I took home-economics classes and learned to sew. About that time, Aunt Agnes began sending us Easter gifts of cash instead of clothing.

We used the money to make our own Easter dresses, picking a pattern we all liked, then buying material that was similar but not matching. At that age, we no longer wanted to be mistaken for triplets.

For years, Aunt Agnes made Easter special. But her generosity did something else: It communicated the joy of giving.

When I became an aunt, and later a great-aunt, I enjoyed shopping for the younger generation. I remember the year I bought sweaters decorated with snowflakes for my grandnieces and grandnephews.

I lovingly packaged the sweaters and sent them off for Christmas. Months later, I found myself wondering if they were appreciated.

Then I thought back to all those Easter dresses and wondered if I'd ever thanked Aunt Agnes. I'm sure our parents had. But what about my sisters and me?

I picked up the telephone. "Aunt Agnes," I said when she answered, "did we ever thank you for the Easter dresses you bought for my sisters and me? If not, I'd like to thank you now."

A moment of silence took us back to those springtimes of years ago. We both choked back tears.

"I don't think you girls ever used those exact words," she said. "But I've been more than rewarded by your love and the fact that we still keep in touch. I enjoyed doing things for you girls because you always appreciated it."

When I hung up, I felt a warm glow. I knew that an outstanding debt of gratitude had finally been paid.

Remember Saying?

cloud 9

Really happy

Fifties Easter Finery

There's nothing like a new hat or dress to help usher in the season of rebirth and renewal. Check out these readers' springtime fashions!

▼ CAUGHT IN THE ACT

This is my brother-in-law, Steve Broussard, displaying his Easter loot in 1953 in his family's yard in Lake Charles. Steve was lucky, with three baskets filled with candy and eggs—and even caught the Easter Bunny at work.

—*Roland Bodin*
Lake Charles, Louisiana

▲ FIVE OF A KIND

For Easter, my mother always made the same dresses for my three girls and my sister Lila's two daughters. She'd walk the girls up to town, in Johnstown, Ohio, to show them off in a sort of miniature Easter parade. My girls have the longer hair and are, from left, Carol, Beth and Barbara. Their cousins are Debbie and Terri Poulos.

—*Kathleen Lewis, Newark, Ohio*

HONEY OF A BUNNY ▶

Little Kerri Reed is all decked out, complete with bunny, for the Easter parade. Kerri's aunt, Lavonne Bouressa of Sacramento, California, vividly remembers those days when she and her sister, Helyn Reed, made colorful Easter outfits for their young daughters.

memories on parade

With its marching bands, royal courts and larger-than-life floats, hometown parades in the 1950s were a spring and summer celebration staple. These reader snapshots will take you back to the spectator sidelines.

FAT TUESDAY

This slide shows my nephew and niece, David and Kitty Hay, all dressed up for the 1952 Mardi Gras promenade in Franklin. The promenade was usually held at the children's school.

—*Roland Bodin, Lake Charles, Louisiana*

MERRY MONTH OF MAY

Remember those lovely May Days when the "Queen of the May" ruled from her flowery throne?

Gretchen Draper of New Hampton, New Hampshire does. She's the charming little brunette seated at right in this photo taken on a chilly first day of May in 1954.

"I was in first grade," she writes. "The teachers chose me to carry the train of the queen's dress when she walked to the stage. People played May Day games and danced around the maypole. I was honored to be such a special part of the festivities."

HERE COMES THE BAND!

This is the 1957 Memorial Day Parade in Portsmouth, New Hampshire.

My stepfather, Al Todd, took this photo from Market Square, looking down Congress Street, Portsmouth's "main drag."

At that time, there were three five-and-dime stores in Portsmouth: W.T. Grant, F.W. Woolworth and J.J. Newberry. The Arcadia Theater (sign above tuba bell) was the first in Portsmouth and originally a nickelodeon.

In the distance, looming over the buildings, two steel structures can be seen. Those are the towers of Memorial Bridge, beyond which are the Portsmouth shipyards.

—*Jackie Schofield, Sacramento, California*

PARADING PRINCESSES

Here I am (*right*), lining up for the annual Auburn Days parade in the summer of 1954. My mother decorated my tricycle with fresh flowers. That's my friend Betty Jo Ewing in front of me, wearing her blue dance costume.

—*Gayle Kroke, Auburn, Washington*

DAFFODIL DELIGHT

When my late husband, Harry Campbell Jr., was in the Army, he was stationed in Fort Lewis, Washington. That's how he came to take these beautiful pictures of the Daffodil Festival parade in 1954.

—*Dorothy Campbell*
Easton, Pennsylvania

coming up roses

Vivian Huff of Bremen, Indiana sent in these photos of the 1956 Rose Bowl Parade. The floats shown here were sponsored by businesses like the Huntington Hotel (woman in dress), Treasure Tone Paints (pirate ship) and Franilla Ice Cream (clown). No doubt they were as elaborate then as they are today.

The parade celebrated the 42nd Rose Bowl game, played on January 2. With 7 seconds left to play, kicker Dave Kaiser won the game against the UCLA Bruins for the Michigan State Spartans and colorful Coach Duffy Daugherty with a 41-yard field goal—final score, 17-14.

Oddly enough, Bruins Coach Red Sanders was quoted in *Sports Illustrated* just a week before, saying, "Winning isn't everything; it's the only thing."

silver screen scare

By Kaye (Cheek) Heath, Rantoul, Illinois

Growing up in Rantoul, Illinois, my sister Helen and I worked at the Home Theater movie theater. As teenagers in the late '50s, there was no better job. We got to go to the movies for free and eat all the popcorn we wanted! On top of that, we were paid 60 cents an hour, and I saw every Elvis movie at least two dozen times.

I worked as an usher, a ticket-taker, in the box office and at the concession stand selling all that wonderful popcorn and candy. Sometimes I was sent to the basement with my little brother, Bobby, to pop corn so that its irresistible aroma drove the moviegoers out of their seats and into the lobby to purchase some.

Some of the fondest memories I have working there are the parties at Halloween. Scary movies were shown at midnight, with the added attraction of "special visitors"—some of the local youth, who put on quite a hair-raising show.

The main street was blocked off. A real hearse stopped in front of the theater and a casket was taken out of the back. Inside was Jannie Patterson, dressed as a lady vampire.

While she was brought onstage in her casket, Rick Gunst, who was the makeup artist as well as the werewolf, made his way through the audience. Suddenly there was screaming as the werewolf jumped over seats, knocking popcorn and soda all over people as they tried to get away.

Joining the ensemble were Dick Ackerman as Dracula, Marcel Lemrise as the mummy, Joe Dullinger as Frankenstein and Patty Patterson as the bride of the monster. They were all as realistic as if they had walked right off the silver screen.

Scary? You bet. A few people ran out of the theater in fear, only to come back after realizing what was going on. Luckily, there were never any casualties. And it was always so much fun to be scared for a little while.

The Home Theater still stands on our main street. Every time I pass by, a happy memory comes back. I have never lost my love of the movies…or that delicious popcorn.

matching holiday best

By Denise Hamilton, Springfield, Ohio

STYLISH SISTERS. Author Denise Hamilton, 4, and sister, Peggy, 6, wore matching outfits at Christmas in 1958 (center photo). A few months later, the two girls donned matching Easter dresses—under their coats (photo right). Denise says, "I love how Peggy and I are holding hands in the pictures...so innocent."

My sister, Peggy, is just over 2 years older than me. When we were little, we had quite a few matching outfits, from pajamas and short-sets to the outfits Mom made of "Ben Casey shirts"—they resembled doctor's white shirts—and blue striped skirts.

Special occasions, of course, called for matching dresses. For Easter in 1959, I still remember we wore matching lavender organdy dresses with big square bib-style white collars trimmed in lace. They were very pretty! My grandmother picked them because lavender was her favorite color. We also wore Easter bonnets and white gloves to attend Easter Sunday church services with my uncle Delbert, aunt Margie and their kids.

Christmas was another occasion for coordinated clothing. In 1958, we were dressed in white blouses, red plaid skirts and saddle shoes. But when we awoke on Christmas morning, our outfits were the farthest thing from our minds.

Peggy and I would wake up early and sneak out into the hallway, where we peeked into the living room to see if Santa had come. Then we'd rush back to our bedroom and debate who would go into Mom and Dad's room to wake them up.

When we went into the living room, there would be so many presents under the tree that they spilled halfway across the room!

Peggy and I always received a doll, and they always came in pairs (although Santa would make sure that they didn't have the same hair color). That Christmas, the dolls came in two cradles and with two identical doll strollers. Other presents included a child-size piano with a bench, stuffed animals, tea sets, assorted toys and some clothes, too.

Give your family a new thrill this Christmas morning
Motorola TV

16 inch TV combination FM/AM radio
—3-speed phonograph. In mahogany
or limed oak.   Model 17F1

Put yourself in this picture by telling your dealer to deliver a Motorola in time for Christmas. Motorola has all the features you want—big, bright pictures—easy operation (just 2 simple controls)—and trouble-free performance (we actually play it at the factory to make sure it works when you get it).

Take your choice of a swell selection of Fashion Award table models, consoles and phonograph combinations—screen sizes from 14 to 20 inches. 29 models, all priced to fit your pocketbook. There's a Motorola for *your* home—*your* budget —*your* family this Christmas. See your Motorola dealer soon.

See your classified directory for the name of your nearest Motorola dealer. Specifications subject to change without notice.

GIVE A MOTOROLA AND YOU KNOW YOU GIVE THE BEST

circa 1950

Oh, Christmas Tree!

By Patricia Carley, Mount Dora, Florida

I took my first teaching job in 1959 in Ludlow, Massachusetts. The school was in a working-class neighborhood of mixed nationalities, including Puerto Rican, Italian and Portuguese.

The adults worked long hours for low pay. My third graders wore hand-me-downs and shared toys with their siblings. For most of their families, a new pencil box or notepad was a major investment.

As the holidays approached, our principal announced that the Lions Club would deliver a Christmas tree to each classroom on a Monday. At the end of the week, each teacher was to choose a deserving student to take the tree home.

When my students heard the news, their faces glowed with joy.

Early Monday morning, we heard a knock on our classroom door. There stood a man holding the scrawniest tree I'd ever seen.

It was obvious our sapling needed to be decorated before the children would settle down, so I gave everyone a job. Joey made paper circles while some of the girls drew angels for decorations. Sammy had saved tin can covers because they resembled shiny balls. Loretta brought wads of cotton to drape over the branches.

When all 30 of us agreed our tree was complete, I asked John, our class president, to plug in the lights. Our little tree shimmered.

Each day that week, the students arrived early to admire their tree. Even some moms and dads managed to come by to see it on their way to work.

Meanwhile, I began worrying about who would take it home.

I decided to turn the problem over to the students themselves; they agreed to decide. I put John in charge of the meeting and left the room.

As I waited, I wondered what they would do. Soon John came out and told me they had reached a solution.

There was a hush as I entered the room. Then, grinning, John announced that every child had voted to give me the tree as my Christmas gift from them!

How could I take the children's beloved tree home when each of them was so needy?

Tears spilled from my eyes. That tree meant so much to each child, yet they were willing to give it to me. I had no choice but to gratefully accept the sacrifice.

Many years have passed, but I've never forgotten the loving little hearts behind that precious gift. Truly, I'd experienced the real meaning of Christmas.

horse rocked his world

By Al Showalterbaugh, Portage, Indiana

I grew up in Merrillville, Indiana with my father, Weber, who worked in the steel mill, and my mother, Frances, who worked hard at raising three children. I had two sisters, Judy, who was 10 years older than me, and Bonnie, 7 years older than me.

In 1951, when I was 4, I got a beautiful white rocking horse for Christmas. My dad had made it with only a file, a hammer and a saw. I loved that horse and named him "Topper" after the white horse ridden by Hopalong Cassidy, a famous cowboy on television at the time.

For years, Topper and I were inseparable. We rode many trails together and rounded up all kinds of bad guys. When I was 8, Bonnie died from leukemia. When my mother told me, I got on Topper and rocked and rocked until we got far, far away!

When I was 19 and my dad had retired, my parents moved to Michigan. My mom gave most of my childhood things to a neighbor boy. Since he didn't want Topper and my parents didn't have room for him, Mom put that well-loved rocking horse out for the garbagemen and watched as they put him on the truck.

Sometimes I still think about Topper and all the miles we traveled together. Giddyap, old friend!

journal entry

Santa left this under my tree!

what a doll

By Peggy Oels, Glendale, Arizona

In December 1959, my family was living in Tucson, Arizona. My father had just started working as a service technician at IBM. His job was in Phoenix, and we stayed with my mother's parents while we waited for our house to be built.

That Christmas, I was 3 and received a Patti Playpal doll from Santa. I was in heaven. She was as big as me and the most beautiful doll in the world.

Years later, as an adult, I was looking at some old slides with my mother, Joan Oels. We got into the Christmas ones and started talking about my Patti Playpal doll. I was astounded when my mother mentioned that the doll had cost $25.

"Twenty-five dollars was a lot of money back then," I said.

"Oh, yes it was," she responded, "but we were just able to manage it."

"Why in the world did you spend that much on a present for me?" I asked.

My mother hit the button on the projector remote and the slide of me delightedly hugging the doll came onto the screen. "That's why," she said simply, smiling at me.

PERFECT PLAYMATE.
Santa left a Patti Playpal doll under the tree for Peggy Oels in 1959…and she couldn't have been more thrilled. Peggy adds, "I am wearing a bridal gown that was a Christmas gift from my mother. She was very handy with a sewing machine and made lovely dress-up gowns for all three of her daughters for Christmas that year."

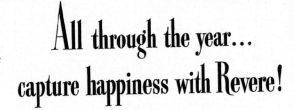

circa 1950

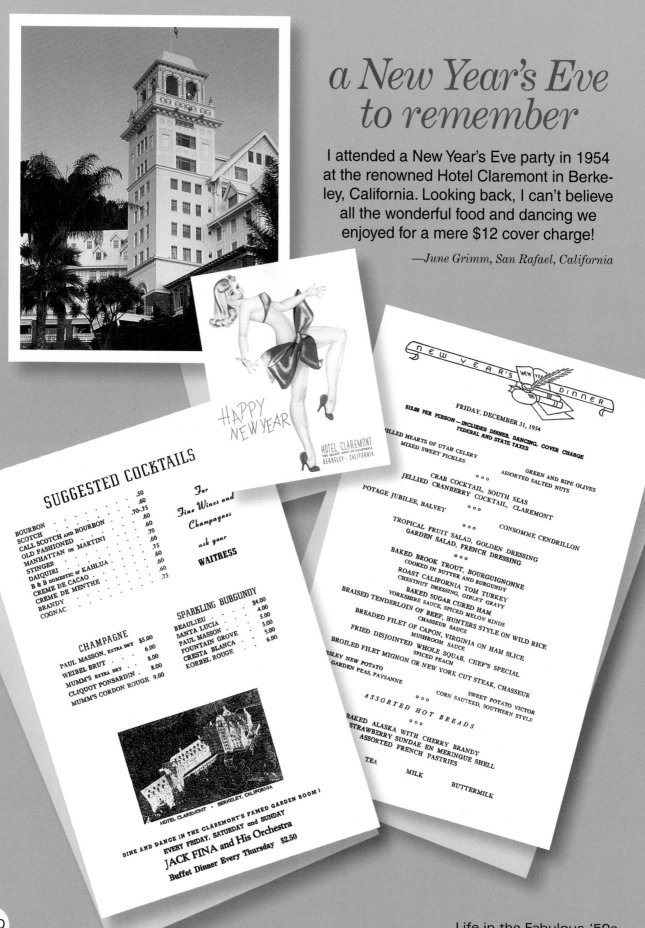

a New Year's Eve to remember

I attended a New Year's Eve party in 1954 at the renowned Hotel Claremont in Berkeley, California. Looking back, I can't believe all the wonderful food and dancing we enjoyed for a mere $12 cover charge!

—*June Grimm, San Rafael, California*

HAPPY NEW YEAR

HOTEL CLAREMONT
THE BEAUTY SPOT OF CALIFORNIA
BERKELEY · CALIFORNIA

SUGGESTED COCKTAILS

BOURBON	.50
SCOTCH	.60
CALL SCOTCH AND BOURBON	.70-.75
OLD FASHIONED	.60
MANHATTAN OR MARTINI	.70
STINGER	.60
DAIQUIRI	.75
B & B DOMESTIC OR KAHLUA	.60
CREME DE CACAO	.60
CREME DE MENTHE	.75
BRANDY	
COGNAC	

For Fine Wines and Champagnes ask your **WAITRESS**

CHAMPAGNE
PAUL MASSON, EXTRA DRY	$5.00
	6.00
WEIBEL BRUT	8.00
MUMM'S EXTRA DRY	8.00
CLIQUOT PONSARDIN	
MUMM'S CORDON ROUGE	9.00

SPARKLING BURGUNDY
	$4.00
BEAULIEU	4.00
SANTA LUCIA	5.00
PAUL MASSON	5.00
FOUNTAIN GROVE	5.00
CRESTA BLANCA	6.00
KORBEL ROUGE	

HOTEL CLAREMONT · BERKELEY, CALIFORNIA

DINE AND DANCE IN THE CLAREMONT'S FAMED GARDEN ROOM!
EVERY FRIDAY, SATURDAY and SUNDAY
JACK FINA and His Orchestra
Buffet Dinner Every Thursday $2.50

NEW YEAR'S DINNER

FRIDAY, DECEMBER 31, 1954
$12.00 PER PERSON — INCLUDES DINNER, DANCING, COVER CHARGE, FEDERAL AND STATE TAXES

CHILLED HEARTS OF UTAH CELERY
MIXED SWEET PICKLES

GREEN AND RIPE OLIVES
ASSORTED SALTED NUTS

° ° °

CRAB COCKTAIL, SOUTH SEAS
JELLIED CRANBERRY COCKTAIL, CLAREMONT

POTAGE JUBILEE, BALVET

° ° °

CONSOMME CENDRILLON

° ° °

TROPICAL FRUIT SALAD, GOLDEN DRESSING
GARDEN SALAD, FRENCH DRESSING

° ° °

BAKED BROOK TROUT, BOURGUIGNONNE
COOKED IN BUTTER AND BURGUNDY
ROAST CALIFORNIA TOM TURKEY
CHESTNUT DRESSING, GIBLET GRAVY
BAKED SUGAR CURED HAM
YORKSHIRE SAUCE, SPICED MELON RINDS
BRAISED TENDERLOIN OF BEEF, HUNTERS STYLE ON WILD RICE
CHASSEUR SAUCE
BREADED FILET OF CAPON, VIRGINIA ON HAM SLICE
MUSHROOM SAUCE
FRIED DISJOINTED WHOLE SQUAB, CHEF'S SPECIAL
SPICED PEACH
BROILED FILET MIGNON OR NEW YORK CUT STEAK, CHASSEUR
PARSLEY NEW POTATO
GARDEN PEAS, PAYSANNE
SWEET POTATO VICTOR
CORN SAUTEED, SOUTHERN STYLE

° ° °

ASSORTED HOT BREADS

° ° °

BAKED ALASKA WITH CHERRY BRANDY
STRAWBERRY SUNDAE EN MERINGUE SHELL
ASSORTED FRENCH PASTRIES

TEA   MILK   BUTTERMILK

Dream Come True

By Sandra L. Lisicki, Estell Manor, New Jersey

In December 1955, I was 7 years old and lived in Cologne, New Jersey. I dreamed about finding a walking bride doll under the Christmas tree. In fact, that is all I thought about—for weeks.

On Christmas morning, my dreams came true. I got my walking bride doll! Even better, my mother, Sophia Schmidt, had made a doll wardrobe out of scraps of material: a dress, a skirt and blouse, a matching hat and coat, a nightgown and even underwear. The nightgown was made from her own wedding-night nightgown. Imagine her cutting that up just for me. What a wonderful mom!

More than 50 years later, I still have my bride doll and her wardrobe. Several years ago, I replaced the rubber bands that make her walk. I also replaced her shoes and headpiece, because the originals were lost through the years. But my joy over this walking dream has never changed.

A BEAUTIFUL BRIDE.
Sandra L. Lisicki shows off her walking bride doll. Also pictured is her dad, Joe Schmidt, who is holding her sister Joann.

A Visit with Santa

For some of us, Christmas just isn't the same without a trip to see a department-store Santa! You know the drill—wait in line for what seems like an eternity…crawl up on the big man's lap…nod your head feebly when he asks if you've been good…and, when it finally comes time to tell him what you want, panic! It's true that such encounters with the bearded man in red have produced many a terrified tot. These readers are adorable exceptions.

◄ CHECKING IT TWICE

Sally Gillespie, right, and fraternal twin, Sue, wore matching outfits when they visited the man in the red suit at Polsky's Department Store in Akron, Ohio in 1955.

Sally writes: "We were 4 years old when this photo was taken. Shortly thereafter, we appeared as two-thirds of the heavenly host in our church's Christmas pageant. Mother made our lovely costumes, and everyone thought we were adorable. I have loved being a twin my whole life. I never minded sharing birthdays, toys or Grandma's lap. Sue has lived as far away as Hong Kong, but we've remained best friends, soul mates and 'womb mates.'"

HE KNEW MY NAME! ►

I look anxious here at age 4, but it's only because I saw my parents, Calvin and Rosalie Ledet, walking down a ramp away from me. I thought they were going to leave me there at Maison Blanche Department Store in New Orleans. I really did want to meet Santa and ask him for a tricycle that Christmas of 1950.

"Susie," he replied, "I think you might rather have a beautiful doll that I have made especially for you." I was amazed he knew my name. And sure enough, I got that doll.
—*Susan Runkles, Houma, Louisiana*

◄ A MAGIC MOMENT

Larry Donnelly, 5, at left, and brother, Dickie, 4, of Arlington, Massachusetts are captivated by Santa at Jordan Marsh department store in Boston in December 1952.

Jeffrey Blout of Stoneham, Massachusetts, a co-worker of the Donnellys at the Arlington Post Office, says, "There is just something about department-store-Santa pictures that captures the innocence of the child and the magic of the season. Notice the look of wonder and enchantment on Dickie's face and the mischief on Larry's as Santa holds his hand. This photo has reduced several people to tears."

house of cards

The tinseled Christmas tree might have been small in this snapshot from Nettie Whitney of Dorchester, Massachusetts, but there was no shortage of friends—judging from the number of cards displayed on the wall.

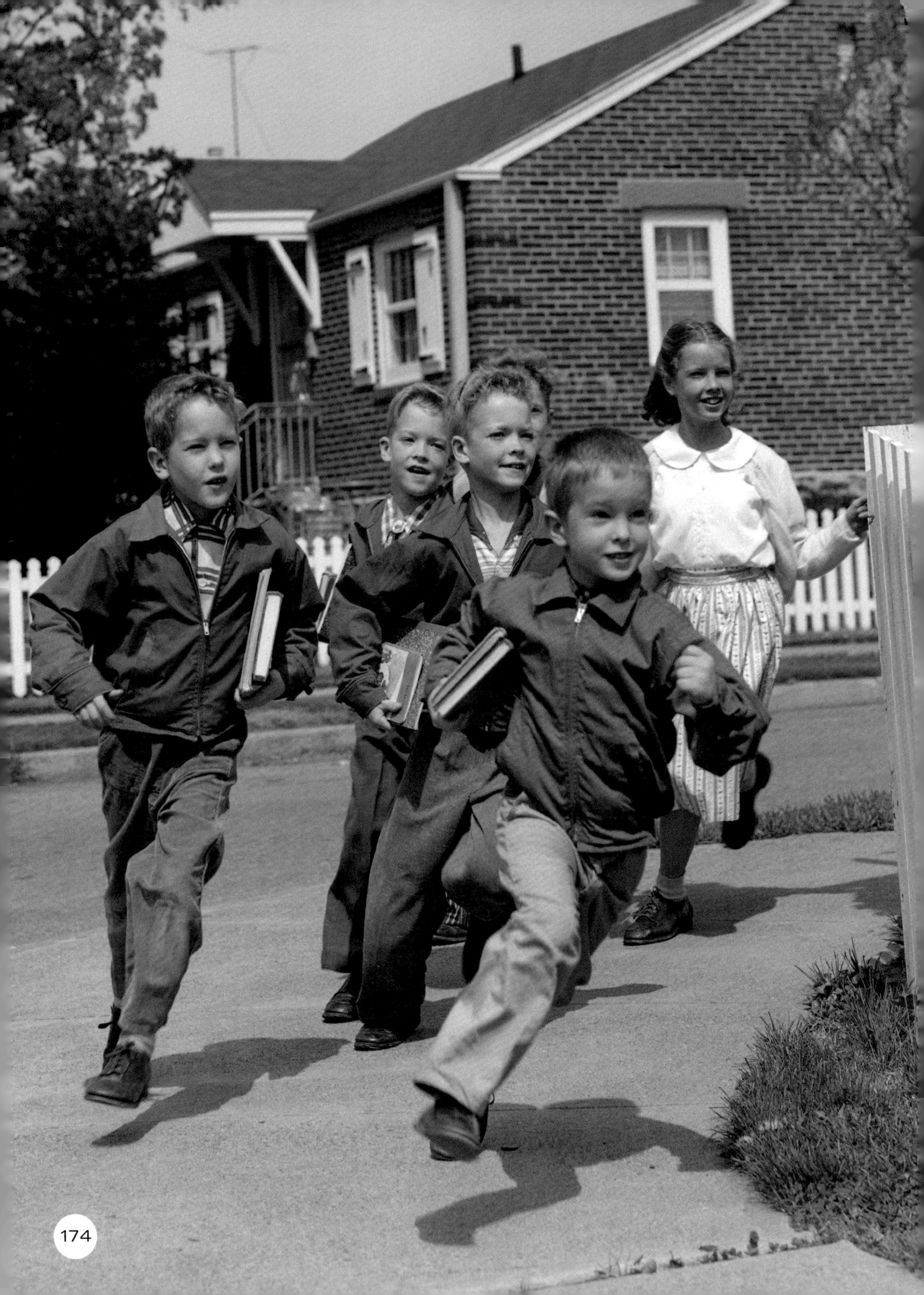

School's in

In the 1950s, social life at West High School in Green Bay, Wisconsin, revolved around jitterbugging the night away at Friday dances, not to mention the occasional formal. For Ann Lee Rioux, the most memorable event was a freshman formal she nearly didn't attend in 1950.

"My parents wouldn't let my sister, Mary Lou, and me go because we didn't have dates," recalls Ann Lee, of Naperville, Illinois. "But then our principal called to tell them everyone goes, even without a date."

That news sent Ann Lee's stepmother scurrying to her Singer treadle sewing machine, where she whipped up two white gowns with red sashes overnight.

"She ran out to buy the material, then stayed up all night," Ann Lee says. "How she did it so quickly, I'll never know."

Ann Lee's dad accompanied his daughters to the formals, departing after taking a spin around the floor with each.

Was her dance card full after Dad left? "Absolutely," she chuckles.

A girl in a new gown will do that.

School was cool in the '50s, as the stories that follow will attest....

Let's Go to the Hop

AFTER SCHOOL, THIS FAMILY-RUN HANGOUT WAS THE PLACE TO BE.

By Kay Dunn, Fillmore, California

My parents, Gene and Lois Griffin, owned and operated the Hickory Hop restaurant from the late 1940s until the late 1970s in the little town of Pico (now known as Pico Rivera), outside East Los Angeles, California.

The Hickory Hop restaurant was a popular hangout for teenagers because it was just down the road from the local high school—El Rancho High School.

It wasn't at all uncommon to welcome carloads of fun-seeking teenagers looking for a friendly place to unwind after a day of classes or a football game. It brought together many friends of my brother and sisters, who worked at the restaurant and attended high school at that time. They could listen to their favorite music and grab a bite to eat.

And since the Hickory Hop offered drive-up service, many times the customers didn't even have to leave the comfort of their '57 »

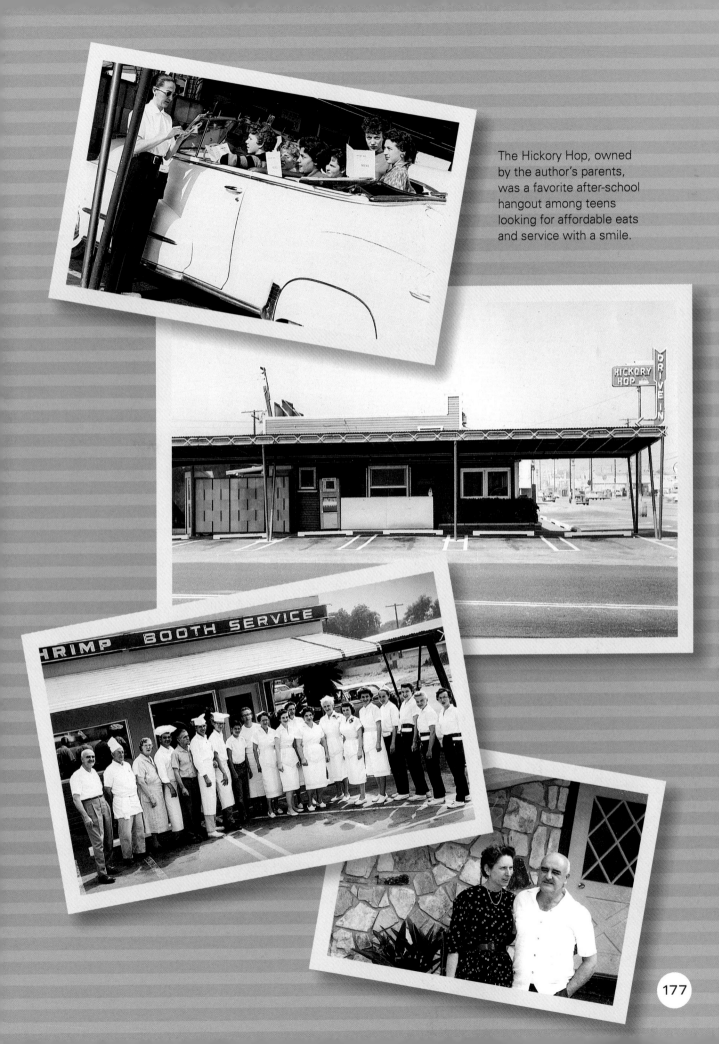

The Hickory Hop, owned by the author's parents, was a favorite after-school hangout among teens looking for affordable eats and service with a smile.

Chevys! All they had to do was to pull into one of the designated parking spaces and a friendly carhop would be out to take their order in a minute or two.

And the prices were right—a hungry teenager could enjoy a burger, fries and root beer float for less than a $1.50. What a deal!

My parents worked very hard and spent many hours at "the Hop," as everyone called it. That's because there was a popular song during the 1950s called *At the Hop*.

The staff who worked there—Bertha, Frenchy, Rascal, Chub and Gidget, just to name a few—were as loyal as employees could be and like family to us.

My father was always cooking for others. He was a cook in the U.S. Marine Corps. He belonged to the Kiwanis for more than 20 years and during charitable events, such as pancake-breakfasts and barbecues, he donated the food and did the cooking.

One of the first rules when the Hickory Hop opened for business was: "If someone was hungry and had no money, they were given soup and coffee." A hobo (that's what we called the homeless in the '50s) once told us that there was a handmade sign at a nearby train track letting the hungry know the way to our restaurant.

My mother was the morning waitress and managed the books. She did payroll once a week. Wages were always paid in cash, which was put into 5-inch envelopes. My three siblings and I spent many hours working there and—like all the employees—we were paid for our time.

The menu featured more than a dozen sandwiches, a dinner menu with steak, shrimp, ribs, ham and roast beef, as well as the Hickory Hop Special—a delicious double-decker hamburger with the fixings and french fries.

The Hop's hamburgers were different from those at other restaurants because they were served on round all-wheat Orowheat grilled bread.

Of course, there were milk shakes, floats, freezes, malts, hot fudge sundaes and ice-cream sodas, too!

Remember Saying?

nuggets
Loose change

HICKORY HOP

DRIVE IN ---

MENU

9342 E. Whittier Blvd.
Pico, California

OXford 5-6111

Fountain Service...

CHOICE OF FLAVORS

Thick Malted Milk 30c	**MILK SHAKES** 30c
TOPPED WITH WHIPPED CREAM	TOPPED WITH WHIPPED CREAM

SUNDAES 30c
TOPPED WITH WHIPPED CREAM
(Chocolate, Pineapple and Strawberry)

HOT FUDGE Sundae 35c

A COOL REFRESHING DRINK
ORANGE or LIME FREEZE 30c

ICE CREAM SODAS 25c
CHOICE OF FLAVORS

Lemonade . 10c -- **Red Lemonade** . 15c

COCA COLA _____ 10c -- ROOT BEER _____ 10c

DISH OF ICE CREAM _____ 15c

ROOT BEER FLOAT _____ 25c

HICKORY HOP
SANDWICH MENU

Hickory Hop Special 65c	**Hickory Burger** 45c **with Cheese** 50c
Double Decker Hamburger, Ham & Cheese, Lettuce, Tomato, Pickle & Dressing & French Fries Onions? It's up to you.	Lettuce, Tomato, Pickle and Dressing. Served on Butter-Toasted Special Orowheat Hamburger Toast. Onions? It's up to you.

Tender Steak Sandwich 85c	**Hot Beef or Ham** 70c
Served with French Fries You'll Like This	MASHED POTATOES and BROWN GRAVY

	.55
PATTY MELT	.55
(Grilled Cheese with a Hamburger Patty)	.55
Bar-B-Q Beef	.30
Bar-B-Q Ham	.30
Cold Beef	.35
Taco	.50
Hot Dog	.30
Grilled Cheese	.50
Bacon & Tomato	.50
Bacon & Avocado	.65
Lettuce & Tomato	.65
Tuna Salad	.30
Chicken Salad	
Fried Ham	
Ham & Cheese	
Ham & Egg	
Fried Egg	

Everything in our Menu can be prepared to take out. So if you are planning a Picnic, Company Drops in, Too Tired or Just Plain Lazy to cook... Just call us... We will have it Ready in a Jiffy.

★ WE RESERVE THE RIGHT TO REFUSE SERVICE TO ANYONE ★

HICKORY HOP
DINNER MENU

SOUTHERN FRIED CHICKEN	$1.35
JUICY STEAK PLATE	1.85
HAMBURGER STEAK PLATE	1.35
JUMBO SHRIMP	1.25
BAR-B-Q RIBS	1.35
ROAST BEEF PLATE	1.35
FRIED HAM PLATE	1.35

ABOVE ORDERS SERVED WITH CHOICE OF SOUP OR CRISP GREEN SALAD, FRENCH OR ROQUEFORT DRESSING, FRENCH FRIED POTATOES, HOT ROLL & BUTTER

LUNCH OR SNACK SUGGESTIONS

Fish & Chips	.70
Burger Size (Onions? It's up to you)	.70
Home Made Chili & Beans	.40
Mulligan Stew	.65
Oyster Stew	.55
Home Made Soup	.20
Mashed Potatoes & Gravy (G.O.P.)	.20
Side Order Buttered Peas	.20
Hash Brown Potatoes	.20
French Fried Potatoes	.35
French Fried Onions	

CRISP GREEN SALAD 30c
French or Roquefort Dressing — Extra dressing 15¢ extra

We make our own French and Roquefort Dressing
It is available to our customers _____75¢ pint

Coffee	10c	Hot Chocolate	20c
Second Cup	10c	Tea	10c
Milk	15c	Pie	20c
Chocolate Milk	20c	Cake	20c

—— NO SUBSTITUTIONS PLEASE ——

high school discoveries

By Earleen Lillegard, Rogersville, Missouri

In the late 1950s, I discovered a lot of things…boys, *American Bandstand*, boys, Hula-hoops, saddle shoes, sweaters with white-starched detachable collars, circle pins, boys, high heels, garter belts, nylons, ponytails, boys, going steady, outdoor theaters and drive-in hamburger stands. Did I mention, BOYS?

Yes, in the '50s, boys were polite and got you home before curfew. Your high school was small enough that you knew the names of all your classmates. Talking in class or chewing gum was the worst infraction a teacher had to deal with. We didn't cheat, steal or skip school. We always wore our clothes neat and clean. The only time you saw above the knee was in gym class.

Conversation at lunch centered on our favorite crooner's newest 45-rpm record. Learning to type was cool, and no one laughed when it was your turn in public-speaking class. We didn't smoke in the bathrooms or run down the hallways. If we borrowed money to buy lunch, we paid it back the next day. Teachers demanded respect…and got it.

If only high school today were as simple as school was back then, what a happier experience it would be for our children.

why school was cool

journal entry

small but swell!

By Rev. Lloyd Running, Yakima, Washington

Living in a small town made for interesting times in high school. I was one of six students in the 1956 graduation class at Frenchtown High School in Frenchtown, Montana. We had just four boys and two girls in our entire class.

We played six-man football throughout our high school years and wore leather helmets. During our senior year, the quarterback was the only one of us who got a fiberglass helmet.

The total high school enrollment was about 35, which enabled us to field a football team with use of lowerclassmen. We did not have the luxury of specializing in one or two sports due to the small number of athletes; we ran track and played football, basketball and baseball.

All of us had our own cars, so we could get home from school after sports practices, which lasted long after the school bus routes had finished.

On a large hill facing the high school, there was a huge "F" or "FHS." Annually, the freshman class was required to climb the hill and whitewash the letters.

CLASSY CROWD. On Frenchtown High School's senior class trip to the Spokane Lilac Festival in Spokane, Washington in 1956 are, from left, Leonard Normand, teacher/sponsor Frank Collins, Monte Peterson, author Lloyd Running, Marvin Jette, clerk/sponsor Doretta Running, Lola Cyr and Donna Mook. "Check out the rolled-up sleeves," comments the author. "They were a style of the times."

In our free time, we had the best fishing and hunting. But most of our social and recreational activities took place in Missoula, which included "dragging the Ave" on Friday and Saturday nights.

At our 50th high school reunion a few years ago, only one member of our class was unable to attend, which I think is amazing. And even more remarkable, all six of us are still married to our original spouses—that's 100 percent of our graduating class! That marriage statistic may not be equaled anywhere!

good times at Larry's

By Margie Roulette Romero, Altadena, California

I was 17 when I started working at Larry's Ice Cream Store in Pasadena, California in 1953. Most of the waitresses dated the neighborhood guys who hung out there. The guys had great motorcycles or cars, were good dancers and were tons of fun to be with. They usually had a choice of four or five girls to date.

All the waitresses wore blue checked blouses and skirts and hung the sale checkbooks on our belts. I worked from 5 to 10 p.m. three times a week, plus Saturday nights, while going to high school and junior college.

As kids, we never had much money, although we could afford a cherry Coke or a burger now and then.

On weekends and in the summer, we would pile into three cars and ride down Colorado Boulevard—the Rose Bowl Parade route on New Year's Day—to meet at a drive-in for burgers, fries, shakes and sodas.

Dick Ahrens drove a souped-up '48 Buick and was always looking for guys to race. We'd arrange a time to meet late at night near the Rose Bowl, where there was a road, few cars and no police. Just the way it was pictured in James Dean's movie *Rebel Without a Cause*, we girls started them off, and they would race for about 50 yards to see who could cross the finish line first.

Then some of us headed up to the hills on the west side of the Rose Bowl to dance. They were just starting to build houses there, so we would find an empty lot, park our cars in a circle, turn off the lights, tune our radios to the same station and dance the night away. When the DJ signed off at 2 a.m., we knew it was time to get home.

One by one, we got married. I married Ruben in 1955. Our bunch got together now and then but eventually became busy with our own lives.

In 1980, one of the gang got cancer, but survived. I said, "That's it. From now on, we're getting together once a month at each other's houses."

Yes, the '50s were the best days of our lives—filled with ice-cream sodas, dancing, young love, long summer nights and music, music, music.

Larry's Ice Cream Store is gone now, but our memories will last forever.

COOL MEMORIES. The author serves a cone to one of the gang at the ice-cream shop (lower left). Her husband-to-be, Ruben, shows off his boots (center) and gives buddies a ride (top).

Remember Saying?

papershaker
Cheerleader

Busted by Burl Ives

By Larry Duckworth, East Alton, Illinois

I grew up in Charleston, Illinois in the 1940s and '50s. I went to school there from elementary through high school and attended college at Eastern Illinois University.

When I was about 10 years old, I decided I wanted to see the college football game that Saturday afternoon after the big homecoming parade. But I didn't have any money for admission.

I knew at one end of the football field there were several trees that hid the 8-foot fence from the view of the field. I quickly climbed the fence and as I dropped to the ground, a man who was in this small woods walked up to me and asked me if I was sneaking into the football game. All I could say was, "Yes." I thought he would put me out, but he just laughed and walked toward the field.

I followed him to the end zone, for that is where I planned to watch the game. He kept walking onto the field and was introduced as Burl Ives. He sang the national anthem, and I never saw him again.

I went home after the game and told the whole story to my mother. She explained to me that Burl Ives had been a college student when she was a young girl and was back in town visiting the college for its homecoming festivities. And then she told me not to sneak into any more football games.

cashing in at the casinos

By Samuel Perroni, Little Rock, Arkansas

Living in Las Vegas in the mid-1950s proved to be a time of lasting memories. Every day, my mother would drive us to take my father to work at the Sands Hotel. When we dropped Dad off, Mom would let us walk past the casinos that graced the Vegas strip: the Moulin Rouge, Flamingo, New Frontier, Desert Inn and Horseshoe Casino. The lights were spectacular—even in the daytime. And once, we got to see Dean Martin and Jerry Lewis perform live at the Sands.

On our walks, I would find coins that people had dropped. In those days, slot machine payoffs were in coins—even silver dollars—and they didn't give people plastic buckets for holding their "mad money," as Mom called it. My haul was usually between 50 cents and $1 each day. That was big money for a 7-year-old!

I loved cowboys, so I used the money I found to buy anything Wild West-inspired. In fact, I'm wearing my favorite cowboy shirt in my second-grade class photo. I loved that shirt. My mother had to fight me to wash it, because I wore it every day until it finally fell apart.

THE WILD WEST. Author Samuel Perroni's second-grade class in Las Vegas, Nevada in 1955. He is the second boy from the left in the back row and is wearing his favorite cowboy shirt.

My school was near our family's home in a small trailer park. If you've ever wondered how young Vegas boys occupied their time at school, the answer is gambling, of course.

During school, we boys would set up little sand alleys with three mounds at one end. On each of the mounds, the "proprietor" would place one large cat's-eye marble. If a "patron" came up, he would shoot a marble from the other end. If he hit the middle cat's-eye, he won all three marbles. If he hit an end marble, he kept it. And if he didn't hit anything, he lost the one he was shooting. I was always a proprietor; the odds were too long as a patron.

But even if a boy had to give up a marble or two, all was not lost. Each week, we were treated to bubble gum! Apparently, a casino manager who was deprived of gum when he was growing up decided to make sure Las Vegas school kids weren't abused the same way. So the manager delivered boxes of gum to our school, and our teacher distributed it to everyone in class. There were bubbles everywhere the days we chewed our gifts of gum.

Out of all the places I lived when growing up—and there were a bunch—Las Vegas still holds the fondest memories for me.

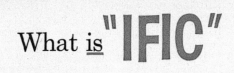

What <u>is</u> "IFIC"

Flavor—freshness—purity, definitions vary.
That's why you won't find the word in a dictionary.
Nonetheless, experts agree, it makes our gum "the most."
A flavor-ific favorite, famous coast to coast.

To find out what "IFIC" really means, chew a
stick of Beech-Nut Gum. Take a flavor-break!

Only 5¢

Beech-Nut Gum is
FLAVOR-IFIC

circa 1958

class act

When Paul Kutta of West Chester, Pennsylvania bought a collection of slides at a church sale in nearby Downington, he found several taken in the mid-1950s of the students and teachers of Franklin Township School in Quakertown, New Jersey.

The slides could have come from a time capsule of school life in the '50s. The kids are seen "ducking and covering" during an air-raid drill. A nutritious hot lunch is being served, and the kids are enjoying their own treats from a variety of colorful lunch boxes and old-fashioned black lunch pails.

Another slide shows a police officer visiting a class to talk about the safety patrol.

And on a big day for the class of 1955, they're seen on a trip to Manhattan, which included a venture to the top of the RCA Building at Rockefeller Center.

These scenes are sure to bring your own classroom memories back to life!

▲ **SAFETY FIRST.** A local police officer met with members of the safety patrol.

▲ **TOP OF THE WORLD.** Class of '55 posed atop the RCA Building in New York City.

▶ **BRING YOUR OWN.** Lunch boxes and thermos bottles made for a good lunch.

▼ **COME 'N' GET IT.** A hot lunch program kept the kids fueled for more learning.

▲ **QUIET PLEASE.**
Students checked out
the reading material in
the school library.

▼ **DUCK AND COVER.**
A few of the kids were
caught peeking during
an air-raid drill in 1954.

a ride down memory lane

By Georgia Buell Adams, Winthrop, Washington

My twin sister, Suzie, and I really had our "happy days" in the latter part of the '50s—especially when our father presented us with a '56 Chevy convertible on our 16th birthday!

We'd begun cheerleading in 1959 for North Kitsap Junior-Senior High School in Poulsbo, Washington—a small town nestled on the shores of Puget Sound.

We enjoyed all the innocent activities of the times—sock hops after the games…Greg's Drive-In for hamburgers, french fries and shakes…the top 10 records on our favorite radio station, KJR…Big Bear Drive-In Theater…"going steady"…and, of course, prom night.

We learned the latest dance steps (to the music of Frankie Avalon, Elvis Presley and Johnny Mathis) by watching *American*

Bandstand. Songs like *Sleepwalk, Venus, Put Your Head on My Shoulder* and *Smoke Gets in Your Eyes* still take us back to those carefree days.

Our most memorable times are reflected in this picture. We're in our '56 Chevy in the homecoming parade, with our brother Nick driving. Suzie is in the center in the backseat, and I'm in front pointing at the crowd on the street.

We'll never forget those happy days. They were the best times of our lives!

deceit at the drive-in

By Marvin Hasson, Boise, Idaho

In 1953, I was attending college at Oklahoma A&M in Stillwater, Oklahoma. One evening, four of my friends and I decided we wanted to go to a drive-in movie. The normal admission charge was 50 cents per person. When we checked our total cash, we had only $1.43. We decided to try to sneak three of us in.

I owned a 1949 Mercury, and it had a fair-sized trunk, so two guys—at 6 feet tall and 180 pounds each—managed to squeeze into it. The third one curled up on the floor between the front and rear seats, and we placed a blanket over him. That left Don and

me in the front seat at 50 cents each. So we still had 43 cents for popcorn. What a plan!

We arrived at the box office with nervous smiles. I handed the lady a dollar bill and drove in, parked and put the speaker in the window. I then waited a bit before I got out and opened the trunk. As the guys (who looked awful) were climbing out of the trunk, the driver in the car behind us turned on his headlights and honked his horn. We were busted.

Then the saint who turned on his lights began to laugh. He told us that during the Wednesday-night special, the price of admission was $1 a carload. We had planned and executed our mission for nothing. That was the reward for cheating.

come dance with me

This picture was taken at a "Coketail" party before a formal during my junior year in 1952 at Holy Angels Academy, a Catholic all-girls school in Milwaukee. My friends and I would meet at somebody's house with our dates, then stop at the academy to visit the nuns. I'm the nervous gal wearing white taffeta, third from left. Our dances were formal—there was a live band and the girls wore gloves with dance cards around their wrists.

—*Kathleen Phillips, Waukesha, Wisconsin*

CHAPTER TEN

Just for Fun

Fun in the '50s didn't require big bucks, says Hal Prey of Greendale, Wisconsin. Good thing, too; in 1950, he was a newlywed, just out of college on the G.I. Bill, and making a meager $50 a week at a Milwaukee radio station.

"Our rent was $10 a week, so money was tight," he says.

But with his wife, Jeanne, Prey managed to conjure up some fun, which often centered on their 1937 Oldsmobile sedan.

"With gasoline at 25 cents a gallon, the vehicle provided cheap entertainment, like Sunday drives to 'window-shop' for dream homes," Prey notes. "It also provided access to drive-in movies.

"A whole carload of people cost just a buck," he says. "And we didn't need to pay a babysitter, because the kids could conk out in the backseat while we watched the movie.

"We hung around with people who were in the same circumstances, so we never felt poor or deprived," he adds. "We were in love and things were going good."

Even on $50 a week.

For even more fun in the fabulous '50s, turn the page....

Westward Ho!

FAMILY ROAD TRIPS WERE AN ECONOMICAL AND EXCITING WAY TO TRAVEL CROSS-COUNTRY IN THE '50s.

By Sandy Perry, Moline, Illinois

LARGER-THAN-LIFE LANDMARKS. The caravan group of 1950 poses in front of Mount Rushmore in South Dakota.

In my grade school years I just loved reading stories of Western life and wished I could have been a cross-country pioneer traveler.

My wish came true in the early 1950s when our family traveled west three times—not in covered wagons, but in car caravans of eight to 18 vehicles.

First organized in the early '30s by Rev. George H. Billings—pastor of Divernon Methodist Church in Divernon, Illinois—these caravans were initially offered to church members but later made available to anyone. The minister's idea was to provide family trips in August for a very modest cost, giving parents and children a chance to enjoy each other's company and see the country at the same time.

DRIVING, CAMPING AND CAMARADERIE

We assembled in Springfield to review the routes and pack the big truck that would carry our tents, cots, bedrolls and tables for the next 2 weeks. Another truck, a refrigerated pickup, carried the perishable foods, propane tanks and cooking supplies.

Each vehicle was numbered on the back with long-lasting Bon Ami soap, and we drove in numerical order to make sure no one was lost. Drivers discussed the weather and the day's route each morning.

Few cars had air conditioning, so we kept the windows rolled down. It was exhilarating to feel the wind blowing through the car, but after a while it was a relief to stop and stretch our legs during our lunch breaks. Sandwiches, fresh fruit and Kool-Aid served in city parks, waysides or parking lots tasted absolutely divine after several long hours on the dusty road.　　　　》

HOMEWARD BOUND. Each trip averaged 2 weeks in August. At the end, families would unpack the caravan trucks, pack up their cars and make their way home.

WELCOME RESPITE. On their 1954 trip, the Buchholz family stopped along the Turner Turnpike near Oklahoma City for sandwiches and milk shakes.

TENT MATES. Burnilda, Pat, and Sandy Buchholz share a tent during a stop in Sayer, Oklahoma during their last caravan trip in August 1954.

SIGHTSEEING. From left to right, Pat, Sandy and Bruce Buchholz in front of the *USS New Mexico* memorial in Santa Fe.

MADE IN NEW MEXICO. This campsite in Hyde Park in the Santa Fe Forest Reserve was 8 miles outside Santa Fe. The Buchholzes' 1950 Nash is in the foreground with "Illinois Caravan, Car #7" written on the back with long-lasting Bon Ami soap.

After lunch our car would leave the caravan to scout out campsites for the night, just like the wagon train scouts of long ago. When the rest of the cars joined us later in the afternoon, the camp bustled as we unloaded the truck, set up the tents and began cooking our evening meal.

The good smells of supper and coffee, plus the sound of a dinner bell, signaled the end of each day. Most nights we'd gather around a campfire to sing hymns and folk songs, tell ghost stories or recount the day's adventures. It wasn't until late that we'd say good night and grope for our cots and bedrolls inside the tents. My mom, Burnilda Buchholz, my older sister, Pat, and I stayed together in one tent while my dad, Leonard, and my brother, Bruce, slept in another tent or in the reclining seats of our 1950 Nash.

We enjoyed the camaraderie of the other travelers while exploring the amazing monuments and magnificent national parks of the Western states. We kids had fun playing together while our parents shared the duties of meals, child care and driving. Our group got lots of attention and press coverage as we traversed the country. Everyone wanted to know how we did it!

LEGENDARY SIGHTS

Dad took hundreds of slides of places like Yellowstone Park, the Grand Canyon, Mount Rushmore, the Corn Palace, Salt Lake City and the Petrified Forest. We walked through Indian homes and climbed the ladders inside Mesa Verde before it was closed to tourists due to its fragility. Our car climbed Pikes Peak easily, while other cars sat in rest areas with their hoods open and steam pouring from the radiators.

SHELL

SECTIONAL MAP OF
SOUTHWESTERN STATES

SHELL

10

Our trips were long, most covering about 4,000 miles round-trip. One trip, as described in a 1954 newspaper article, took us from Springfield to Kansas City, Missouri; Mesa Verde, Colorado; Gallup, New Mexico; Flagstaff, Arizona and the Grand Canyon; Albuquerque and Santa Fe; and then back through Amarillo, Texas; Oklahoma City and St. Louis.

In 1955 my parents bought a farm that required all our time and money. Vacations were limited to visiting relatives. Our years of caravanning were over, but the memories remain in the slides, journals and brochures that Dad packed away.

journal entry

my most memorable
road trip

Photo courtesy of James Nix, Holley, NY

it's a gas!

When gas prices were this low, travel by car (even in those '50s gas guzzlers) was a real no-brainer. Read 'em and weep….

1952 — 27¢ a gallon
1956 — 23¢ a gallon
1957 — 31¢ a gallon
1958 — 30¢ a gallon

"Hey! We almost forgot the most important thing!"

Remember to remember **your** camera this weekend. And for beautiful snapshots in color–load it with Kodacolor Film

All good times just naturally "happen" in color. So why not catch them that way . . . in Kodacolor snapshots . . . to enjoy over and over again.

Kodacolor snapshots are every bit as easy to take as black-and-whites. And how they sparkle! Look at the pictures on this page, for example. See how brilliant the colors are? You can have your Kodacolor snapshots processed locally in many cities, or processed by Kodak. Just ask your dealer.

See Kodak's "The Ed Sullivan Show" and "The Adventures of Ozzie and Harriet."

EASTMAN KODAK COMPANY, Rochester 4, N. Y.

Kodak
TRADEMARK

sunday fun day!

A group from our church took a Sunday drive to this lake in northern Wisconsin in the summer of 1952. I took this picture of my gang and my 1950 Lincoln convertible. I was 21 at the time, working as a printer's apprentice, and I believe I was probably trying to court one of the young ladies in the car.

—*Bob Crawford, Apple Valley, Minnesota*

home is where the fun is

Whether playing cards with the neighbors or enjoying an evening with the family, these readers prove that in the 1950s, a good time could be found just beyond the welcome mat.

SOFA SLEEPERS. My good friend Nina—now Mrs. Ed Murray of Searcy, Arkansas—took this picture at one of our slumber parties when she and I shared a flat during the early '50s in St. Louis. We enjoyed entertaining our friends. It looks like we wore ourselves out on this particular evening.

—Mildred Beehner
Doniphan, Missouri

GAME ON. Board games like Scrabble, Yahtzee and Tactics were popular in the '50s. But remember Carrom?

"Carrom is a parlor game played by the whole family. The two-sided square board features a checkers side and crokinole side," says Jimmy Rosen of Duncannon, Pennsylvania. "My family acquired the manufacturer in 1981, and we still produce many of the old-time favorites like Nok-Hockey, Skittles and Bowl-A-Mania."

POKER FACES. Taken Dec. 30, 1950, at the home of Helen and Adolph P. Heisdorf after the wedding of their daughter, Bernice, this picture shows Carl Koehler, Carl Rahn and the uncle of the bride, Raphael Reding, enjoying cigars, cocktails and a friendly game of cards.
—*Jerome A. Heisdorf*
Elkhart Lake, Wisconsin

COFFEE KLATCHERS. In 1955, all the ladies in our Winchester, Massachusetts neighborhood got together for a coffee klatch on a regular basis, taking turns as hostess. My mother, Jean Stafford, is sitting on the floor in her lounging pajamas. She was pregnant with my sister Kim.
—*Norma Jean Hissong*
Olympia, Washington

drive-ins were a great night out

Back in the '50s, a night on the town often meant heading to the drive-in. What else could a young married couple afford, and what could be more romantic than sitting in a parked car in the dark alongside a dreamy guy or gal?

GOOD TIMES WITH THE FAMILY

"Before TV, we entertained ourselves with drive-in movies on Saturday night.

"In the '50s, we had a big family and money was scarce. We'd pop a big bag of popcorn and fill a jug with Kool-Aid, then pile in our car—admission was just $1 a carload. A night at the drive-in was something we looked forward to every week."

—*Kathryn McGaughey, Denver, Colorado*

Classicstock.com

HOW EMBARRASSING!

Drive-in movies proved fertile ground for some embarrassing moments. D.D. Giles of Grants Pass, Oregon tells of the time she and her friend Mary double-dated in an old beige Chevy.

"During the movie, Mary's date, Chuck, walked to the snack bar. On the way back, he jumped into the passenger side of another Chevy that looked just like ours," D.D. explains. "Then he handed the popcorn to 'Mary.'

"'Who are you?' asked a strange voice in the darkness. Startled, Chuck realized he was in the wrong car and leaped out. I don't think he and Mary ever had another date!"

DISASTER IN THE DARK

Benjamin Bello of Totowa, New Jersey became the victim of a classic drive-in mishap in 1953. "We were leaving at the end of the show when I noticed the driver alongside me had forgotten to unhook the speaker from his car," Benjamin recalls.

"As the speaker cord stretched to its full length, it snapped and shot back like a missile, crashing into my headlight. To the guy's credit, he stopped and gave me $15 for the damage."

Benjamin also remembers the pre-show game of "tag" the audience would play. "Someone would shine a spotlight on the blank screen and see if anyone else with a spotlight could 'catch' them," he says. "It resulted in a dazzling light show."

THREE LITTLE WORDS

"Because they were so private, each couple at the Saturday drive-in could share a tender moment that was theirs alone. There they could whisper those three little words, 'I love you.'

"Drive-in movies are mostly gone now, but the memory of those innocent, incurably romantic days will always live on."

—*Lorraine Ranieri, Mantua, New Jersey*

journal entry

my memorable drive-in moments

rodeo royalty

By Jean (Dwinell) Poss, Elba, Nebraska

In July 1952, I turned 17 and had recently graduated from high school. My friend Bernice Willard surprised me by sending our names to the Burwell Rodeo Board to become queen contestants for Nebraska's Big Rodeo in Burwell. When she told me, I couldn't believe it! I had never been to the Big Rodeo, and we were so thrilled to be accepted! But there was a problem.

Although I lived on a ranch and we had many horses, none was suitable for a rodeo queen contestant to ride. Bernice's dad offered me one of their horses to ride. It was a beautiful, well-mannered white horse, and I just loved it. For $1.98, I bought myself a red Variety Store hat and enjoyed the next 4 days.

Because we lived about 50 miles away, Bernice and I stayed in Burwell with friends. Our horses stayed in the barns on rodeo grounds. Each morning, we would take care of the horses and ride around Burwell—through the park and back to the rodeo grounds where we rode in the Grand Parade, sat in the box seats for the queen contestants and enjoyed the rodeo.

Each evening, we were in our box seats enjoying the evening events. We wore our arm bands very proudly showing that we were a part of the big event. I'll never forget it.

Miami Dream

By Temple Pouncey, Georgetown, Texas

In 1955, my aunt, Merrill Pouncey Combs, and her husband, Reese Combs, invited me to spend the summer with them.

Excited to leave Texas for the very first time, I arranged for someone to cover my paper route and boarded a bus for the 44-hour ride from Dallas to Miami. Sitting in the front seat across from the driver, I relished my first look at such cities as New Orleans and Tallahassee. When we motored into the heart of Florida, we were greeted by orange-juice stands in splashy bright oranges and reds, and an endless chain of palm trees.

Miami was a dream place for a summer, not least because my aunt and uncle had built a comfortable bungalow in the exclusive suburb of Bay Point, with postcard views of Miami Beach. I lived in the guesthouse behind the porte cochere. The front lawn was lavish with soft green grass.

On weekdays, Aunt Merrill drove me across the causeway to the Bath Club. The doorman and I compared notes on how the Brooklyn Dodgers were doing—on the way to their first World Series championship.

At the club, my aunt played canasta while I swam in the ocean and ordered soft drinks up to her cabana. They came in tall glasses with a cherry on a stem, and all I had to do was sign for them. This was a long way off from life for this 13-year-old in Dallas.

When we motored into the heart of Florida, we were greeted by orange-juice stands in splashy bright oranges and reds...

Even then, Miami was a bilingual city. As I walked around downtown, I saw signs reading, "No seas una bota-basura" ("Don't be a litterbug") and my favorite, "Sonrie, porque la vida en Miami es un sueño" ("Smile, because life in Miami is a dream").

The summer of '55 didn't last nearly long enough, but I was fortunate enough to pay a return visit in 1956.

That was the year the great pitcher Leroy "Satchel" Paige came to play for Bill Veeck's Miami Marlins. One night, we drove to the old Miami Stadium and saw how colorful and effective a 50-year-old former big leaguer could be.

That was my last summer in Miami. Today, the little bungalow on Sable Palm Drive has made way for a grander home behind guarded gates. The Bath Club still operates on Collins Avenue, but I suspect it's a little tougher to reserve a cabana these days.

Nevertheless, memories of Miami in the '50s linger like a tropical breeze.

Coney Island skies

John Heller of Lakewood, Colorado took
this photograph of the parachute jump at Coney Island,
New York on a September day in 1958.
It was so windy that day that John remembers
a parachute getting hung up on the scaffolding! The riders
were suspended high in the air until help arrived.

MUDDY BUDDIES
My daughter, Judy (left), and niece, Joan (right), are having a great time in 1955 playing in the sand near Johnson Lake in Lexington, Nebraska. To be a kid again!
—*Maxine Scheschy*
Carter Lake, Iowa

HOT DOG!
Sand and sausage made a winning combination for our then 3-year-old son Rick at this summer outing at Lake Erie in 1952. Here he's enjoying a beach barbecue and doing a great job roasting a hot dog on a stick.
—*Arthur and Louella Kightlinger*
Erie, Pennsylvania

PERFECT PICNIC
With the sound of the surf in the background and the warm sun on their backs, the Held family picked the perfect spot to picnic in the summer of 1956. Submitted by Nancy Castles of Coral Springs, Florida, the scenery in this slide comes courtesy of Dennisport on Massachusetts' Cape Cod.

Just Beachy at Rockaway

By Maureen Reid, Little Silver, New Jersey

As someone who grew up in Manhattan in the '50s, I can recall the steam rising from the blacktop and the stifling heat inside our apartment building when temperatures rose above 100 degrees in summer.

My family was one of the fortunate few that escaped the city for cooler comfort in a large boarding house in Rockaway Beach, Queens, New York. We didn't own a car, so we left for our retreat from the 96th Street subway station.

Every year, the same families returned to the house from the end of June until Labor Day. The parents reacquainted themselves and the children rekindled the friendships that lay dormant in winter.

Our fathers commuted to work each day by train. I remember one father in particular. Every evening upon returning to the house, he—collar open, tie undone, sleeves rolled up to the elbows, sweat pouring from his forehead—would remind us how lucky we were to enjoy such a lavish vacation: "Would you believe it was 105 in the city today? Do you know how fortunate you are to spend the entire summer by the ocean?"

The accommodations were strictly no frills; usually one small room would sleep a family of four, with a community bathroom down at the end of the hall, minus a bathtub. The outside shower was in back of the house. And with 40 or more tenants using it, one knew not to linger.

In the community kitchen, each family had an assigned table and a shelf in the pantry and refrigerator for their food. Many times a kid would deliberately snatch something from the wrong shelf, knowing full well his mother would never buy such a tasty snack.

The best treat was at the end of the year when the owner of the house, Mr. Cassidy, would throw a Labor Day party in the basement. He would treat all the mostly Irish-American boarders to corned beef and cabbage, along with all the tasty bread and boiled potatoes we could eat!

circa 1953

Mountain Memories

By Sandra Kendrick Huggins, Mesa, Arizona

For 10 years, my dad rented a pop-up camper or tent every summer in July for 2 weeks. My family and I took it along as we headed out for our favorite campground in the Smoky Mountains of North Carolina.

My mother worked hard sewing our new vacation clothes, scrimping and saving all year for this special time.

We lived in Florida, so mountains were intriguing to us. The excitement began in north Georgia—from then on it was "Let's see who spies a mountain first!"

When we arrived, my dad chose our campsite. Then we'd venture into town for firewood and groceries from the A&P. We had a camp stove but preferred cooking over an open fire, especially if marshmallows were involved.

Around the campfire, we'd plan our day trips to Cherokee Village, Pigeon Forge and the Biltmore home and gardens in Asheville. And, of course, there were many days of swimming in the creek and hiking in the mountains with my younger brother.

Our last trip was the summer I turned 16. I had no idea how much I would yearn for those mountains and lazy days 40 years later.

I've had several opportunities to return to that campground as an adult. Though each trip has been wonderful, I've never been able to recapture the excitement of the 10-year-old girl who exclaimed, "I see the mountains!"

the way we were

Here's a snapshot of my mom, Norma Brown,
and me taken in the summer of 1952 on vacation
at the Grand Canyon. I have many pictures from family trips,
but I cherish this one the most.

—*Jan Brown Buker, Titusville, Florida*